What the reviewers

"The daring account of a strong-willed woman who defeated poverty, racism, alcohol and drug addiction by the age of thirty-three."

— *Saturday Night*

"Here speaks a voice never heard before with such direct frankness, such humour: the voice of the true Canadian woman."

— Novelist Rudy Wiebe, author of
The Temptations of Big Bear

"You can almost feel this book vibrating in your hands, it is so compelling. You read it with a kind of agonized, heart-in-the-mouth sensation, halfway between laughter and tears. . . . Truth is stronger than fiction."

— Victoria *Times-Colonist*

"Sometimes a book tells us what we have always known but in a way that makes it seem as if we have not heard it before."

— *The Toronto Star*

"Powerful, simple, direct, and passionate without being bitter."

— CBC Radio Vancouver

This book is dedicated to my Cheechum's children. Thank you Stan Daniels for making me angry enough to write it; Peggy Robbins, for your understanding and encouragement but especially for believing I could do it; my family, for your patience; Elaine, Kay, Sheila, Sarah and Jean, for understanding, listening, typing and babysitting; and a special thank-you to my friend Dianne Woodman.

HALFBREED

Maria Campbell

GOODREAD BIOGRAPHIES

Copyright © 1973 by Maria Campbell.
All rights reserved.
This book may not be reproduced in whole or in part, by
mimeograph or any other means, without permission.
For information, write to McClelland and Stewart Limited,
Suite 900, 481 University Avenue, Toronto, Ontario, M5G 2E9.

CANADIAN CATALOGUING IN PUBLICATION DATA

Campbell, Maria.
Halfbreed

ISBN 0-88780-116-1

1. Campbell, Maria.   2. Métis — Canada, Western —
Biography.*   I. Title.

E78.C2C23 1983   971.2'00497   C83-099191-3

Published in 1973 by McClelland and Stewart Limited
Published in a Seal Books edition in 1979
Published in 1983 by Goodread Biographies
Canadian Lives series publisher: James Lorimer

Goodread Biographies is the paperback imprint of
Formac Publishing Company Limited
5502 Atlantic Street
Halifax, Nova Scotia
B3H 1G4

The house where I grew up is tumbled down and overgrown with brush. The pine tree beside the east window is dried and withered. Only the poplar trees and the slough behind the house are unchanged. There is a family of beavers still there, busy working and chattering just as on that morning, seventeen years ago, when I said good-bye to my father and left home.

The graveyard down the hill is a tangle of wild roses, tiger lilies and thistle. The crosses are falling down and gophers scurry back and forth over the sunken graves. The old Roman Catholic church still needs repainting but because of the poverty of the congregation it continues to wait until another year.

The blacksmith shop and cheese factory across the road have long since been torn down and only an old black steam-engine and forgotten horseshoes mark the place where they once stood. The store is still there, old and lonely, looking like the country around it, and, like the people it serves, merely exists. The French owners who came from Quebec are dead and their families have gone. It is as if they were never there.

Grannie Campbell's house is gone. The Halfbreed families who squatted on the road allowances have moved to nearby towns where welfare hand-outs and booze are handier, or else deeper into the bush as an

1

escape from reality. The old people who were so much a part of my childhood have all died.

Going home after so long a time, I thought that I might find again the happiness and beauty I had known as a child. But as I walked down the rough dirt road, poked through the broken old buildings and thought back over the years, I realized that I could never find that here. Like me the land had changed, my people were gone, and if I was to know peace I would have to search within myself. That is when I decided to write about my life. I am not very old, so perhaps some day, when I too am a grannie, I will write more. I write this for all of you, to tell you what it is like to be a Halfbreed woman in our country. I want to tell you about the joys and sorrows, the oppressing poverty, the frustrations and the dreams.

Chapter 1

In the 1860's Saskatchewan was part of what was then called the Northwest Territories and was a land free of towns, barbed-wire fences and farm-houses. The Halfbreeds came here from Ontario and Manitoba to escape the prejudice and hate that comes with the opening of a new land.

The fear of the Halfbreeds that their rights would not be respected by the Canadian government when it acquired the land from the Hudson's Bay Company, along with the prejudice of the white Protestant settlers, led to the Red River Rebellion of 1869. Louis Riel established a provisional government at Fort Garry, Manitoba, but escaped to the United States in 1870 when troops arrived from eastern Canada.

So with their leaders and their lands gone, the Halfbreeds fled to the areas south of Prince Albert, Saskatchewan, and established the settlements of Duck Lake, Batoche, St. Louis and St. Laurent. There was no government in Saskatchewan at the time and no law and order, so they formed their own, fashioned after their way of life—the order and discipline of the great Buffalo Hunts. They elected Gabriel Dumont as their president, and with him eight councillors. They set up laws by which the people could live peaceably, and penalties if the laws were broken. They made it clear that they weren't opposed to the Canadian government and would abandon their council as soon as the Territories acquired a true government and was able to establish law and order.

Here, for a very few years they lived happily, but the 1870's and 1880's brought the settlers and the railroad, and just as had happened in Ontario and Manitoba their way of life was again threatened. They were squatters with no title to the land they lived on. They wanted assurance from Ottawa of their right to keep the land before the incoming white settlers encroached on them by using homestead laws. Our people believed the lands acts discriminated against them, stating that they had to live on the land and wait three years before filing a claim. They had lived on the lands for years before the lands acts had ever been thought of, and didn't believe they should be treated like newcomers. They sent many petitions and resolutions to Ottawa but again, as in Ontario and Manitoba, Ottawa was not interested and continued to ignore their existence.

Finally, in 1884, they decided to ask the only man who could help them. Gabriel Dumont and three of his councillors rode to Montana to see Louis Riel who was living in exile. Riel returned with them to Saskatchewan to discover that it was not only Halfbreeds who had reasons to complain but white settlers and Indians as well. Because of pressing demands in the east, Macdonald's Conservative government had cut federal monies going to the Territories. This left the Indians without the rations and farming assistance promised to them under the treaties. The white settlers had suffered one disaster after another including three years of drought—this, together with their dissatisfaction over the lands claims acts, had completely soured them against the federal government.

This time petitions and resolutions went to Ottawa from white settlers, Halfbreeds and Indians. Again Ottawa ignored them. The Halfbreeds by now were angry and ready to take up arms but Riel and the white settlers didn't want a rebellion. Riel believed there had to be a more peaceful way to make Ottawa realize the urgency of their requests. Dumont, however, had no faith in the federal government—he believed only an armed rebellion would give them what they asked for. He urged Riel to seize Fort Carlton and to declare a provisional government as he had done at Fort Garry in Manitoba. Finally Riel took Dumont's advice and established a provisional government. He gave the North West Mounted Police at the Fort an ultimatum—to surrender or they would attack. Meanwhile, Dumont had gathered together a party of armed Halfbreeds and Indians, and without Riel's knowledge approached the Fort. Crozier, the NWMP officer in charge of the Fort, had sent to Regina for reinforcements when he received Riel's ultimatum. However, on seeing Dumont and his party approaching, Crozier decided, very foolishly, to take his inexperienced troops out against Dumont's skilled sharpshooters.

This was the Battle of Duck Lake, a victory for the Halfbreeds, and was the beginning of the Riel Rebellion. The majority of white settlers didn't want violence and withdrew their support after Duck Lake, but the treaty Indians, who were starving because of Ottawa's broken promises, supported Dumont and Riel. Poundmaker and Big Bear, chiefs renowned as warriors and respected throughout the Territories, brought their warriors to join forces with the Halfbreeds.

After Duck Lake, Ottawa hastily formed a committee to examine Halfbreed grievances and issued land scripts to assure the Halfbreeds of their land claims. But these were issued purposely to a chosen few which caused a split within the Halfbreed ranks. Had the committee been formed earlier, the Battle of Duck Lake and the Riel Rebellion would never have happened.

Meanwhile, eastern troops under General Middleton were being sent to Saskatchewan. The CPR line had not been completed and troops and supplies had to be transported on sleighs between unfinished points. Within a month, eight thousand troops, five hundred NWMP and white volunteers from throughout the Territories, plus a Gatling gun, arrived to stop Riel, Dumont and one hundred and fifty Halfbreeds.

The history books say that the Halfbreeds were defeated at Batoche in 1884.

> Louis Riel was hanged in November of 1885. Charge: high treason.
>
> Gabriel Dumont and a handful of men escaped to Montana.
>
> Poundmaker and Big Bear surrendered, were charged with treason, and sentenced to jail for three years.
>
> The other Halfbreeds escaped to the empty pockets of North Saskatchewan.
>
> The total cost to the federal government to stop the Rebellion was $5,000,000.

Chapter 2

My people fled to Spring River* which is fifty miles north-west of Prince Albert. Halfbreed families with names like Chartrand, Isbister, Campbell, Arcand, and Vandal came here after the Riel Rebellion where the men had been actively involved. Riel was gone now and so were their hopes. This new land was covered with small lakes, rocky hills and dense bush. The Halfbreeds who came were self-sufficient trappers and hunters. Unlike their Indian brothers, they were not prepared to settle down to an existence of continual hardship, scratching out a scanty living from the land. They were drawn to this part of Saskatchewan because the region was good for hunting and trapping, and there were no settlers.

In the late 1920's the land was thrown open for homesteading and again came the threat of immigrants. By this time the lakes were drying up and the fur and game had almost disappeared. Having nowhere else to go, nearly all the families decided to take homesteads so that the land would belong to them. It was difficult to accept the fact that times were changing, but if there was to be a future for their children, the roaming, free life must be forgotten.

The land was ten dollars for a quarter section. Ten acres had to be broken in three years, along with improvements, before title would be granted. Other-

---

* Names of persons and places have been changed in some cases.

wise the land was confiscated by Land Improvement District authorities. Due to the depression and shortage of fur there was no money to buy the implements to break the land. A few families could have scraped up the money to hire outside help but no one would risk expensive equipment on a land so covered with rocks and muskeg. Some tried with horse and plough but were defeated in the end. Fearless men who could brave sub-zero weather and all the dangers associated with living in the bush gave up, frustrated and discouraged. They just did not have the kind of thing inside them that makes farmers.

Gradually the homesteads were reclaimed by the authorities and offered to the immigrants. The Halfbreeds then became squatters on their land and were eventually run off by the new owners. One by one they drifted back to the road lines and crown lands where they built cabins and barns and from then on were known as "Road Allowance people."*

So began a miserable life of poverty which held no hope for the future. That generation of my people was completely beaten. Their fathers had failed during the Rebellion to make a dream come true; they failed as farmers; now there was nothing left. Their way of life was a part of Canada's past and they saw no place in the world around them, for they believed they had nothing to offer. They felt shame, and with shame the loss of pride and the strength to live each day. I hurt inside when I think of those people. You sometimes see that generation today: the crippled, bent old grandfathers and grandmothers on town and city skid rows; you find them in the bush waiting to die; or baby-sitting grandchildren while the parents are drunk. And there are some who even after a hundred years continue to struggle for equality and justice for their people. The road for them is never-ending and full of frustrations and heart-break.

---

* Road Allowance: crown land on eiher side of road lines and roads.

I hurt because in my childhood I saw glimpses of a proud and happy people. I heard their laughter, saw them dance, and felt their love.

A close friend of mine said, "Maria, make it a happy book. It couldn't have been so bad. We know we are guilty so don't be too harsh." I am not bitter. I have passed that stage. I only want to say: this is what it was like; this is what it is still like. I know that poverty is not ours alone. Your people have it too, but in those earlier days you at least had dreams, you had a tomorrow. My parents and I never shared any aspirations for a future. I never saw my father talk back to a white man unless he was drunk. I never saw him or any of our men walk with their heads held high before white people. However, when they were drunk they became aggressive and belligerent, and for a little while the whites would be afraid of them. Even these times were rare because often they drank too much and became pathetic, sick men, crying about the past and fighting each other or going home to beat frightened wives. But I am ahead of myself so I will begin again and tell of Dad's family.

Great Grandpa Campbell came from Edinburgh, Scotland, with his brother. They were both tough, hard men, and on the boat to Canada they got into a fight and disowned each other. They settled in the same area, both married native women and raised families. Great Grandpa married a Halfbreed woman, a niece of Gabriel Dumont. Prior to the marriage both brothers had wanted the same woman, and although Great Grandpa won, he was convinced that his only child was his brother's son and so he never recognized Grandpa Campbell as his own, nor did he ever speak to his brother again during his lifetime.

He ran a Hudson's Bay store just a few miles west of Prince Albert and traded with the Halfbreeds and Indians around that area. When the Northwest Rebellion broke out in 1885, he was involved with the North West Mounted Police and the white settlers. He was not well-liked by his neighbours or the people who traded with him. Our old people called him "Chee-pie-hoos," meaning "Evil-spirit-jumping-up-and-down." They say he was very cruel and would beat his son, his wife, and his livestock with the same whip and with equal vengeance.

Grandpa Campbell ran away from home once when he was about ten His father found him and tied him beside his horse. The old man then climbed in the buggie and whipped both the horse and Grandpa all the way home.

He was also a very jealous man and was sure his wife was having affairs with all the Halfbreeds in the area. So when the Rebellion broke out and he had to attend meetings away from home he would take his wife with him. She in turn passed on all the information she heard at these meetings to the rebels and also stole ammunition and supplies for them from his store. When he found out he became very angry and decided the best way to deal with her was by public flogging. So he stripped the clothes from her back and beat her so cruelly she was scarred for life.

He died not long after. Some people say her family killed him, but no one knows for sure. His wife went to her mother's people who lived in what is now known as Prince Albert National Park. Even though they were Indians they were never part of a reserve, as they weren't present when the treaty-makers came. She built a cabin beside Maria Lake and raised her son. Years later when the area was designated for the Park, the government asked her to leave. She refused, and when all peaceful methods failed the RCMP were sent. She locked her door, loaded her rifle, and when they arrived she fired shots over their heads, threatening to hit them if they came any closer. They left her alone and she was never disturbed again.

I remember her as a small woman, with white hair always neatly braided and tied with black thread. She wore black, ankle-length full skirts and black blouses with full sleeves and high collars. Around her neck were four or five strings of bright beads and a chain made of copper wire. On her wrists were copper bracelets which she wore to ward off arthritis. She wore moccasins and tight leggings to emphasize her tiny ankles. These were covered with bright porcupine quill designs.

Great Grandma Campbell, whom I always called "Cheechum," was a niece of Gabriel Dumont and her whole family fought beside Riel and Dumont during the Rebellion. She often told me stories of the Rebellion and of the Halfbreed people. She said our people never wanted to fight because that was not our way. We never wanted anything except to be left alone to live as we pleased. Cheechum never accepted defeat at Batoche, and she would always say, "Because they killed Riel they think they have killed us too, but some day, my girl, it will be different."

Cheechum hated to see the settlers come, and as they settled on what she believed was our land, she ignored them and refused to acknowledge them even when passing on the road. She would not become a Christian, saying firmly that she had married a Christian and if there was such a thing as hell then she had lived there; nothing after death could be worse! Offers of relief from welfare were scorned and so was the old age pension. While she lived alone she hunted and trapped, planted a garden, and was completely self-sufficient.

Grandpa Campbell, Cheechum's son, was a quiet man. No one remembers him too well, as the old people who are alive now seldom saw him or his wife. Grannie Campbell was a small woman with black curly hair and blue eyes. She was a Vandal, and her family had also been involved in the Rebellion. I cannot remember her ever saying very much and I never heard her laugh out loud. After their marriage, they lived miles out in the bush and never bothered much with anyone. Grandpa Campbell was a good friend of

Grey Owl, an Englishman who came to our land and lived as an Indian. Grandpa loved the land and took from it only what he needed for food. Daddy says he was a kind, gentle man who spent a great deal of time with his children. He died when he was still young, leaving nine children, the oldest of whom was Daddy, aged eleven.

After Grandpa died, Grandma Campbell went to a white community and hired herself and Dad out to cut brush for seventy-five cents an acre. She wrapped their feet with rabbit skins and old paper, and over this they wore moccasins. They would put on old coats, then drive by horse and sleigh to work. Dad says that some days it would be so cold he would cry, and she would take the skins from her feet and wrap them around him and continue working.

In the spring after the farmers had broken the brushed land, they would return and pick the stones and roots and burn the brush, as the farmers wouldn't pay the seventy-five cents an acre until all this was completed.

In the fall they went to work harvesting. They did this until they had enough money to buy a homestead. She and Dad built a cabin and for three years tried to break the land. Because they only had one team of horses and Dad used these to work for other people, Grannie on many occasions pulled the plough herself. After three years of back-breaking work they still weren't able to meet the improvements required, so they lost title to the land. They moved then to the Crown lands along the road lines, and joined other "Road Allowance people."

As Daddy and his brothers grew older, they trapped, hunted, and sold game and homemade whiskey to the white farmers in the nearby settlements. When they each were married, they built their cabins beside Grandma's.

Grannie Campbell had a special place in our hearts. Daddy loved her a great deal and treated her with special tenderness. She was a very hard worker and it seemed as though she worked all the time. When Daddy tried to make her stop, as he could have looked after her, she became quite angry and said he had a family to worry about and what she did was none of his business. She brushed and cleared the settlers' land, picked their stones, delivered their babies, and looked after them when they were sick. Her home was always open to anyone in the community who cared to drop in, but in the forty years she lived there no white people ever visited her home, and only three old Swedes came when we buried her.

Daddy married when he was eighteen. He went to a sports day at the Sandy Lake Indian Reserve, saw my mother, who was then fifteen, wanted her and took her. He was a very good-looking man with black curly hair and blue-grey eyes, strong, rowdy and wild. He loved to dance and was dancing when Mom first saw him, his moccasined feet flashing in a Red River jig. Dad first saw Mom cooking bannock over a fire outside her parents' tent. She flipped the bannock over just like his mother did. When she looked up he nearly fell off the wagon she was so pretty. He told me that he asked some people about her and learned she was Pierre Dubuque's only daughter and he'd best leave her alone or the old man would shoot him. Daddy said Mom had many admirers, the most ardent of these a Swede from a nearby community who had a large farm and lots of money. Dad said he made up his mind he was going to marry Mom, and that night he noticed Mom liked to dance, so he danced as hard as he could, hoping she would notice him. Mom said she saw him and knew she belonged with him. I remember Dad being the same when I was a little girl— warm, happy, always laughing and singing, but I saw him change over the years.

My Mom was very beautiful, tiny, blue-eyed and auburn-haired. She was quiet and gentle, never outgoing and noisy like the other women around us. She was always busy cooking or sewing. She loved books and music and spent many hours reading to us from a collection of books her father gave her. I grew up on Shakespeare, Dickens, Sir Walter Scott, and Longfellow.

My imagination was stirred by the stories in Mom's books. In good weather my brothers and sisters and I gathered our cousins behind the house and organized plays. The house was our Roman Empire, the two pine trees were the gates of Rome. I was Julius Caesar and would be wrapped in a long sheet with a willow branch on my head. My brother Jamie was Mark Anthony, and shouts of "Hail Caesar!" would ring throughout out settlement. Other times we would build a raft with logs and put a bright patchwork quilt canopy over it, with Mom's bright scarves flying from the four corners. An old bearskin rug was laid down and Cleopatra would go aboard. She was our white-skinned, red-haired cousin.

Oh, how I wanted to be Cleopatra, but my brother Jamie said, "Maria, you're too black and your hair is like a nigger's." So, I'd have to be Caesar instead. Cleopatra's slaves would all climb aboard and we'd push the raft into the slough and I as Caesar would meet it on the other side and welcome Cleopatra to Rome. Many times poor Cleo and her slaves came to a bad end for the logs would come apart and they would fall into the water. Then the Senators (our mothers) would fish everyone out and we would have to do something else. Many of our white neighbours who saw us would ask what we were playing and would shake their heads and laugh. I guess it was funny—Caesar, Rome, and Cleopatra among Halfbreeds in the backwoods of northern Saskatchewan.

Mom laughed often in those early years, but I remember mostly the clean, spicy smell when she held me close and sang to me at night. She had a soft voice and sang and crooned the babies to sleep.

Mom's parents were very different from Dad's

family. Grandma Dubuque was a treaty Indian
woman, different from Grannie Campbell because
she was raised in a convent. Grandpa Dubuque was a
huge, strong-willed Frenchman from Dubuque, Iowa.
His grandfather had been a *coureur de bois* and had
been given a land grant in Iowa by the Spanish king.
There the family mined ore and started a lumber in-
dustry and founded the city of Dubuque. Grandpa
came to Canada and arranged his marriage with
Grannie through the nuns at the convent. Mom was
their only daughter and when she was five years old
they sent her to a convent to be educated.

Grandpa wanted her to marry a gentleman and
live like a lady. He was heart-broken when she ran off
with Dad. And to add to his disappointment she was
on the trapline in early spring when I was born. However, he finally gave them his blessing at the marriage
six months later.

Chapter 3

I was born during a spring blizzard in April of 1940. Grannie Campbell, who had come to help my mother, made Dad stay outside the tent, and he chopped wood until his arms ached. At last I arrived, a daughter, much to Dad's disappointment. However this, didn't dampen his desire to raise the best trapper and hunter in Saskatchewan. As far back as I can remember Daddy taught me to set traps, shoot a rifle, and fight like a boy. Mom did her best to turn me into a lady, showing me how to cook, sew and knit, while Cheechum, my best friend and confidante, tried to teach me all she knew about living.

I should tell you about our home now before I go any further. We lived in a large two-roomed hewed log house that stood out from the others because it was too big to be called a shack. One room was used for sleeping and all of us children shared it with our parents. There were three big beds made from poles with rawhide interlacing. The mattresses were canvas bags filled with fresh hay twice a year. Over my parents' bed was a hammock where you could always find a baby. An air-tight heater warmed the room in winter. Our clothes hung from pegs or were folded and put on a row of shelves. There were braided rugs on the floor, and in one corner a special sleeping rug where Cheechum slept when she stayed with us, as she refused to sleep on a bed or eat off a table.

I loved that corner of the house and would find

any excuse possible to sleep with her. There was a special smell that comforted me when I was hurt or afraid. Also, it was a great place to find all sorts of wonderful things that Cheechum had—little pouches, boxes, and cloth tied up containing pieces of bright cloth, beads, leather, jewelry, roots and herbs, candy, and whatever else a little girl's heart could desire.

The kitchen and living room were combined into one of the most beautiful rooms I have ever known. Our kitchen had a huge black wood stove for cooking and for heating the house. On the wall hung pots, pans and various roots and herbs used for cooking and making medicine. There was a large table, two chairs and two benches made from wide planks, which we scrubbed with homemade lye soap after each meal. On one wall were shelves for our good dishes and a cupboard for storing everyday tin plates, cups and food.

The living-room area had a homemade chester-field and chair of carved wood and woven rawhide, a couple of rocking chairs painted red, and an old steamer trunk by the east window. The floor was made of wide planks which were scoured to an even whiteness all over. We made braided rugs during the winter months from old rags, although it often took us a full year to gather enough for even a small rug.

There were open beams on the ceiling and under these ran four long poles the length of the house. The poles served as racks where furs were hung to dry in winter. On a cold winter night the smell of moose stew simmering on the stove blended with the wild smell of the drying skins of mink, weasels and squirrels, and the spicy herbs and roots hanging from the walls. Daddy would be busy in the corner, brushing fur until it shone and glistened, while Mom bustled around the stove. Cheechum would be on the floor smoking her clay pipe and the small ones would roll and fight around her like puppies. I can see it all so vividly it seems only yesterday.

17

Our parents spent a great deal of time with us, and not just our parents but the other parents in our settlement. They taught us to dance and to make music on the guitars and fiddles. They played cards with us, they would take us on long walks and teach us how to use the different herbs, roots and barks. We were taught to weave baskets from the red willow, and while we did these things together we were told the stories of our people—who they were, where they came from, and what they had done. Many were legends handed down from father to son. Many of them had a lesson but mostly they were fun stories about funny people.

My Cheechum believed with heart and soul in the little people. She said they are so tiny that unless you are really looking for them you will never find them; not that it matters, because you usually only see them when they want you to.

The little people live near the water and they travel mostly by leaf boats. They are a happy lot and also very shy. Cheechum saw them once when she was a young woman. She had gone to the river for water in the late afternoon and decided to sit and watch the sun go down. It was very quiet and even the birds were still. Then she heard a sound like many people laughing and talking at a party. The sounds kept coming closer and finally she saw a large leaf floating to shore with other leaves following behind. Standing on the leaves were tiny people dressed in beautiful colours.

They waved to her and smiled as they came ashore. They told her that they were going to rest for the evening, then leave early in the morning to go further downstream. They sat with her until the sun had gone down and then said good-bye and disappeared into the forest. She never saw them again, but all her life she would leave small pieces of food and tobacco near the water's edge for them which were always gone by morning. Mom said it was only a fairy tale but I would lie by the waters for hours hoping to see the little people.

Cheechum had the gift of second sight, although she refused to forecast anything for anyone. Once in a while if someone had lost something she would tell them where to find it and she was always right. But it was something over which she had no control.

Once, when we were all planting potatoes and she and I were cutting out the eyes, she stopped in the middle of a sentence and said, "Go get your father. Tell him your uncle is dead." I ran for Dad, and I can remember word for word what she told him. "Malcolm shot himself. He is lying at the bottom of the footpath behind your mother's house. I'll prepare the others. Go!" (Malcolm was Dad's brother-in-law.) Dad took off, with me right behind him. When we reached Grannie Campbell's no one was home. While Dad went to the door I sped down the footpath. Just as Cheechum had said, my uncle's body was lying there just as if he was sleeping.

Another time, late at night, Cheechum got up and told Dad that an aunt of ours was very sick and that he should go for Grannie Campbell as there was no time to waste. They arrived a few minutes before the aunt died.

She often had this kind of foresight and would tell Mom and Dad days before someone died or something happened. I wanted to be able to see things as she did, but she would reply that it was a sad thing to know that people who are close to you are going to die or have bad fortune—and to be unable to do anything to help them because it is their destiny. I am sure that she could see what was in store for me but because she believed life had to take its course she could only try to make me strong enough to get through my difficulties.

Qua Chich was Dad's aunt, Grannie Campbell's older sister, a widow, and a strange old lady. She had mar-

ried Big John when she was sixteen. He had come to
the Sandy Lake area before it was made a reserve. He
brought with him two yoke of oxen, an axe and a
beautiful saddle horse. He settled beside the lake,
built himself a large cabin and broke the land. After
the first year there was a home, a crop, a garden, and
the saddle horse had a colt. He traded one ox for a
cow and a calf, the other for another horse, and then
went hunting for a wife.

He visited all the nearby families and looked over
their daughters, finally settling on Qua Chich because
she was young and pretty, strong and sensible. Some
years later, when the treaty-makers came, he was
counted in and they became treaty Indians of the
Sandy Lake Reserve instead of Halfbreeds. Then the
great flu epidemic hit our part of Saskatchewan
around 1918 and so many of our people died that mass
burials were held. Big John went first and a week later his two children.

Qua Chich never remarried; half a century later
she still wears widow's clothes: long black dresses,
black stockings, flat-heeled shoes and black petticoats
and bloomers. She even wore a black money-bag fastened with elastic above her knee, as I discovered one
day when peeking under the tent flaps. A small black
bitch, blind in one eye from age, went everywhere
with her. She scolded it continually, calling it bitch in
Cree and accusing it of running around shamelessly
with the other dogs.

She was considered wealthy by our standards as
she owned many cows and horses as well as a big two-
storey house full of gloomy black furniture. She was
stingy with money, and if someone was desperate
enough to ask for help she would draw up formal pa-
pers and demand a signature.

Qua Chich visited her poor relations, the Halfbreeds, every year in early May and late September.
She would drive up to our house in a Bennett buggy

pulled by two black Clydesdales and set up her own tent for a week. The first afternoon she would visit Mom and Dad. Her black eyes never missed anything and when she focused them on us we would fairly shrink. Sometimes I would catch her watching me with a twinkle in her eye but she would quickly become her usual self again.

The second day of her visit she would rouse Dad and my uncles out of bed early so that they could take her horses to plough and rake our large gardens. In the fall we could haul our supply of wood for the winter. When this was done, she would rest the horses for a day and then go on to visit other relatives. Our people never had strong horses and few had good ploughs, so this was her way of helping. When one of the family married she gave them a cow and a calf, or a team, but the calf was usually butchered the first year and the cow often suffered the same fate. The horses just ended up as Halfbreed horses—fat today, skinny tomorrow.

Once a year we all went to Qua Chich's house, usually when the cows came fresh. She would line the young ones all around the table and bring a pudding from her oven made from the first milking. She would say a prayer in Cree before we ate that awful pudding, and then we were not allowed to talk or make a sound all day, which was very difficult for us noisy, rowdy children. Dad said he had to do this too when he was little.

Once the old lady told me never to look at animals or people when babies were being made or else I would go blind. Of course, this was repeated with great authority among the rest of the kids. About a week later one of my boy cousins looked at two dogs and screamed that he was blind. By the time we helped him to the house we were all hysterical. Cheechum finally calmed us down and found out what had happened. She told us all to be quiet and said, "No

21

one goes blind from seeing animals make babies. It is a beautiful thing. Now stop being so foolish and go and play."

When World War II broke out many of our men were sent overseas. The idea of travelling across Canada was unbelievable enough, but the sea was frightening for those who had to let loved ones go. Many of our men never returned, and those who did were never the same again. Later on, I'd listen to them talk about the far-off places I'd read about in Mom's books, but I never heard any of them talk about the war itself.

Daddy signed up but was rejected, much to his disappointment and everyone's relief, especially Chee-chum's. She was violently opposed to the whole thing and said we had no business going anywhere to shoot people, especially in another country. The war was white business, not ours, and was just between rich and greedy people who wanted power.

We also acquired some new relatives from the war: war brides. Many of our men brought home Scottish and English wives, which of course didn't go over very well with our people. They marry either their own kind or Indians. (It is more common among Indians to marry a white.) However, these women came and everyone did their best to make them welcome and comfortable.

What a shock it must have been for them to find themselves in an isolated, poverty-stricken, native settlement instead of the ranches and farms they had believed they were coming to!

Two of the war brides I remember very well. One was a very proper Englishwoman. She had married a handsome Halfbreed soldier in England believing he was French. He came from northern Saskatchewan's wildest family and he owned nothing, not even the shack where a woman and two children were waiting for him. When they arrived, his woman promptly beat the English lady up and gave her five minutes to get

out of her sight, and told the man she'd do what the
Germans didn't do (shoot him) if he didn't get his ass
in the house immediately. Mom brought the woman
home and because she had no money and too much
pride to write home and ask for some,. the people in
the settlement got together and collected enough
money to pay her way to Regina, where they were
sure the government would help her. She wrote Mom
a letter from England a year later and was fine.

The other bride was a silly blonde. She married a
sensible hard-working man who provided well for her,
but she drank and ran around, and was so loud and
bawdy that she shocked even our own women. In
spite of everything she was kindhearted and likeable,
and eventually settled down to raise a large family.

I grew up with some really funny, wonderful, fantas-
tic people and they are as real to me today as they
were then. How I love them and miss them! There
were three main clans in three settlements. The Arcands were a huge group of ten or twelve brothers
with families of anywhere from six to sixteen children
each. They were half French, half Cree, very big men,
standing over six feet and over two hundred pounds.
They were the music-makers, and played the fiddles
and guitars at all the dances. We always knew, when
arriving at a party, if there was an Arcand playing.
They were loud, noisy, and lots of fun. They spoke
French mixed with a little Cree. The St. Denys, Ville-
neuves, Morrisettes and Cadieux were from another
area. They were quiet, small men and spoke more
French than English or Cree. They also made all the
home brew, of which they drank a lot. They were *ak-
ee-top* (pretend) farmers with great numbers of poor
skinny horses and cows. Because they intermarried a
great deal years ago, they looked as scrubby as their
stock.

The Isbisters, Campbells, and Vandals were our
family and were a real mixture of Scottish, French,

23

Cree, English and Irish. We spoke a language completely different from the others. We were a combination of everything: hunters, trappers and *ak-ee-top* farmers. Our people bragged that they produced the best and most fearless fighting men—and the best looking women.

Old Cadieux was always having visions. Once he saw the Virgin Mary in a bottle when he was pouring home brew, and prayed for a week and threw all his booze out, much to everyone's dismay. The priest had given his daughter a bottle with the Virgin inside to try to scare him out of making home brew and she had put it beside the other empty bottles. Poor old Cadieux! He was very religious and never missed Mass, but he was back making booze again in a week. He made what we called *shnet* from raisins, yeast bran, old bannock and sugar. He kept it in his cellar where we once saw a swollen rat floating in it. He just scooped it out and strained the brew. His wife was a French woman who spoke no English and was almost too fat to move. One daughter, Mary, was tiny, with one of the most beautiful faces I ever saw. She was very religious and wanted to become a nun.

In the Cadieux family was Chi-Georges, son of Old Cadieux. He was short and round with extra-long, skinny arms. He was near-sighted and slow-witted and always drooled. He walked everywhere because he didn't trust horses, and wherever he went he had a bannock under his arm. When he got tired he would climb up a tree, sit on a branch and eat his bannock. If someone asked what he was doing up there he would say, "Hi was jist lookin' 'round to see hif hi could spot a hindian. Don't trust dem hindians!" It was nothing out of the ordinary to go somewhere and see Chi-Georges up in a tree.

He died some years ago after a party with his father. He had been missing for six days when Pierre Villeneuve, out setting rabbit snares, came running to the store all bug-eyed and screaming in French, "He's

laughing at me!" The men in the store followed him
and found Chi-Georges lying on a footpath with his
head on a fallen tree, his eyes and mouth pecked off
by birds. His whole body was moving with maggots.
Poor Pierre, who was the local coward, prayed for
months, and if he had to go anywhere at night he always carried a rosary, a lantern, a flashlight and
matches so he would have a light. He was afraid Chi-
Georges would haunt him.

Then there were our Indian relatives on the
nearby reserves. There was never much love lost between Indians and Halfbreeds. They were completely
different from us—quiet when we were noisy, digni-
fied even at dances and get-togethers. Indians were
very passive—they would get angry at things done to
them but would never fight back, whereas Halfbreeds
were quick-tempered—quick to fight, but quick to forgive and forget.

The Indians' religion was very precious to them
and to the Halfbreeds, but we never took it as seri-
ously. We all went to the Indians' Sundances and special gatherings, but somehow we never fitted in. We
were always the poor relatives, the *awp-pee-tow-
koosons*.* They laughed and scorned us. They had
land and security, we had nothing. As Daddy put it,
"No pot to piss in or a window to throw it out." They
would tolerate us unless they were drinking and then
they would try to fight, but received many sound beatings from us. However, their old people, "Mush-
ooms" (grandfathers) and "Kokums" (grandmothers) were good. They were prejudiced, but because
we were kin they came to visit and our people treated
them with respect.

Grannie Dubuque's brother was chief on his reserve and as they loved me, I often stayed with them.
Mushoom would spoil me, while Kokum taught me to
bead, to tan hides and in general to be a good Indian

---

* Awp-pee-tow-koosons: half people.

woman. They had plans for me to marry the chief's son from a neighbouring reserve when we grew up. But the boy was terrified of me and I couldn't stand him.

They took me to pow-wows, Sundances and Treaty Days, and through them I learned the meanings of those special days. Mushoom would also take me with him to council meetings which were always the same: the Indian agent called the meeting to order, did all the talking, closed it and left. I remember telling Mushoom, "You're the chief. How come you don't talk?" When I expressed my opinion in these matters, Kokum would look at Mushoom and say, "It's the white in her." Treaty Indian women don't express their opinions, Halfbreed women do. Even though I liked visiting them, I was always glad to get back to the noise and disorder of my own people.

Chapter 4

The immigrants who came and homesteaded the land were predominantly Germans and Swedes. On small farms they raised pigs, poultry, a few cows and a bit of grain. I remember these people so well, for I thought they must be the richest and most beautiful on earth. They could buy pretty cloth for dresses, ate apples and oranges, and they had toothbrushes and brushed their teeth every day. I was also afraid of them. They looked cold and frightening, and seldom smiled, unlike my own people who laughed, cried, danced, and fought and shared everything. These people rarely raised their voices, and never shared with each other, borrowing or buying instead. They didn't understand us, just shook their heads and thanked God they were different.

During Christmas they would drive by all the Halfbreed houses and drop boxes off at each path. Dad would go out, pick up the box and burn it. I cried, because I knew it contained cakes and good things to eat, and clothing that I had seen their children wear. This was always a bad day for Dad as he would be very angry, and Mom would tell me to be very quiet and not ask questions. Our neighbours all wore this cast-off finery, and as I got older and started school I was glad Daddy had burned the clothes because the white girls would laugh when my friends wore their old dresses and say, "Mom said I should put it in the box as my Christian duty." By the time I reached the age of ten I had the same attitude as Cheechum about Christians, and even today I think of Christians and old clothes together.

All our people were Roman Catholic, but at that time we had neither a priest nor a church. Mom was happy when the Germans built their church. They were Seventh-Day Adventists and worshipped on Saturday. She wasn't pleased with this but overlooked it, sure that God would understand and forgive her for attending. The important thing was to go to church.

In spite of Dad's pleading and Cheechum's disapproval and wrath, I was dressed up and taken with Mom in the wagon. She had told me so much about God and churches that I was fairly jumping out of my too-tight shoes. We arrived late and as we walked in the minister saw us and stopped talking, so everyone turned and looked at us. There was no place to sit except in the front pew, where Mom knelt down and started to say her rosary. A lady leaned over and said something to her, whereupon Mom took my hand and we left. We never went back and it was never discussed at home.

The men used to tell of the only time an Evangelist minister came to our part of the country to try to civilize us. He was a Saint-Denys. He had been saved from a life of sin by the Evangelists and now he was coming back to do the same for his people.

In the community lived an old, old man called Ha-shoo, meaning Crow. He was a Cree Medicine Man. Ha-shoo loved to chant and play the drum. When Saint-Denys arrived he asked some young men to go about the settlement and tell people about the church services. When the messenger arrived at Ha-shoo's house, the old man asked, "What do they do?" The boy said, "Oh, Grandfather, they talk and sing." The old man answered, "I'll be there and I'll bring my drum."

So to the service he went. The minister conducted it in Cree with lots of hollering and stamping. Finally he said, "Now we will sing." Old Ha-shoo, who was sitting on the floor, took up his drum and began to chant. The minister yelled, "Ha-shoo, you son-of-a-bitch! Get the hell out of here!" The old man got up and left, and so did the rest of the congregation.

When I was still quite young, a priest came to hold masses in the various homes. How I despised that man! He was about forty-five, very fat and greedy. He always arrived when it was mealtime and we all had to wait and let him eat first. He ate and ate and I would watch him with hatred. He must have known, because when he finished eating all the choice food, he would smile at me, rub his belly and tell Mom she was a great cook. After he left we had to eat the scraps. If we complained, Mom would tell us that he was picked by God and it was our duty to feed him. I remember asking why Daddy didn't get picked by God. All through my childhood years that priest and I were enemies.

Eventually our people were able to build a church and two nuns came to keep house for the priest. We were all baptized and I had to go to catechism. What a drag that was! The nuns would never answer our questions and all we did was pray and pray until our knees were sore. The churchyard, which was the graveyard as well, was just down the hill from our house and it had the most luscious strawberries in the country. However we weren't allowed to pick them. The berries, said the Father, belonged to the Church, and if we took them it would be stealing from God. This made us very angry. We had seen him many times taking things from the Indians' Sundance Pole, and that belonged to the Great Spirit. So my brother Robbie and I decided one day to punish him. We took Daddy's rabbit wire and strung it across two small green trees on either side of the footpath. The wire was tight as a fiddle string.

We strung more wire a couple of feet further down the path and then hid in the bushes. It was almost dusk. Soon the Father came striding down the path, tripped on the first wire and fell to the ground, moaning. He scrambled up, only to hit the second wire and crash head first to the ground again. There was silence for a few seconds and then he started to curse. Robbie and I by this time were doubled over trying to smother our laughter. But when we looked up and saw Father heading for our hiding place, we were frightened out of our wits. We knew he would whip us so we ran home as fast as we could. Mom and Daddy were sitting at the table drinking tea when we entered. We pretended nothing had happened and went quietly off to bed without the usual argument. A few minutes later the Father arrived. We sneaked over to the door and heard Momma ask him in for a cup of tea but he refused. It was difficult to overhear their conversation until the priest raised his voice and we heard him say, "I'm sorry for you. I guess all we can do is pray."

"My wife and my kids don't need your goddam prayers," Dad shouted. "Now get the hell out!" We scrambled back to bed and pretended to be fast asleep, but Dad hauled us out by the scruff of our necks. He demanded to know what we had done and why. Forgetting that we were supposed to be innocent, we told him the whole story about the strawberry patch and the Father stealing from the Sundance Pole. Dad got a funny look on his face and Mom became very busy at the stove. He sent us to bed, but when morning came we were whipped with a razor strap and told that regardless of what the Father had done, it was not our job to punish him. Years later, Daddy told us that Mom had prayed for a week afterwards because she had laughed so much. The Father never dropped by again to eat our Sunday dinners and we left the strawberry patch to God.

There were several churches in our part of the country besides the Roman Catholic ones—the Lutheran which the Swedes built and later abandoned, the Church of England (Anglican), the Seventh-Day Adventists and the Holy Rollers. The Roman Catholic and Anglican buildings were frame with steeples and bells, and were whitewashed inside and out. The yards were kept clean and trim by the native people in the community who believed that if they didn't keep it neat they would roast in hell. The Catholic churches were beautiful with waxed hardwood floors and pews, many tall statues and paintings of the Stations of the Cross. The Protestant churches were long, one-roomed log structures, grey with age and dusty inside, their yards overgrown with brambles and weeds. They had small congregations of white people.

In general the Halfbreeds were good Catholics and the Masses were always well attended regardless of weather or circumstances, because missing Mass was a mortal sin. We could break every commandment, however, during the week and be quite confident that the worst that could happen would be to say a few "Hail Mary's" when we went to confession.

The Mass was held in Latin and French, sometimes in Cree. The colourful rituals were the only thing which made the church bearable for me. I was spellbound by the scarlets and purples and even the nuns, whom I disliked as persons, were mystical and haunting in their black robes with huge, swinging crosses. They reminded me of "The Lady of Shallot" floating down the river. My imagination would run wild in Mass and with eyes shut as in prayer, I would dream of far-off places. The pomp and pageantry would take me to Egypt and England and the Knights of the Round Table. Then Mom would poke me and I would come to with a start, and there would be just the old priest and the little altar boy in front of us.

Our people talked against the government, their white neighbours and each other, but never against the church or the priest regardless of how bad they were. No one, that is, except Cheechum, who hated them with a vengeance. I used to wonder why my mother was not even critical, because surely if a little girl could see the fat priest for what he was, then she could. But she accepted it all as she did so many things because it was sacred and of God. He was not just any God either, but a Catholic God. Cheechum would often say scornfully of this God that he took more money from us than the Hudson's Bay store.

The reserves near our home were all Catholic except for the Sandy Lake Reserve, which was a Church of England stronghold. The Ahenikews, Starblankets and Birds, well-off and educated families, were the most powerful members, and were always the chiefs and councillors. One or two of the Ahenikews became ministers and some of the women married ministers.

The church on the Reserve was built beside the lake and had a beautiful interior which was lovely, but not as elaborate as the R.C. church in our settlement. When I visited Mushoom and Kokum, I went to services with them. My imagination was even more inspired here because the Catholic nuns always told us that this church was founded by fornicators and adulterers. In answer to my questions about this, Mom said that the reasons lay with Henry VIII, a wicked king who had had to build a new church so that he could divorce his wives and marry others. Even though I was supposed to think of him as a wicked, sinful man, I rather liked him because he was an exciting figure, but I was disappointed that he belonged to the Indians instead of the Halfbreeds.

By the time I was four, I had two brothers. But I was still number one in Dad's eyes as Jamie was quiet and docile and Robbie was too young to be competition. However, when Jamie was six and Robbie four, they began to take over my place with Dad. At the age of seven I was kept home with Momma and the old ladies while my brothers went with Dad to the store and to the homes of his friends. I became very resentful and jealous and did all sorts of things to attract attention.

One occasion stands out very clealy in my mind. Sunday afternoons were a real highlight in our lives because of the baseball games. After church and dinner, Daddy would hoist me up behind the saddle and away we'd go. This particular Sunday I rushed around as usual after dinner getting changed when Robbie appeared all dressed up in a blue sailor's suit with a white collar. Dad said to me, "Maria, it's his turn today, Jamie's next Sunday, then the Sunday after that will be your turn."

I was so stunned I couldn't think for a moment, but there were no tears as Dad had always told me, "Campbells never cry." I was sitting outside sulking when Mom asked me to take Robbie to the outhouse. This was in May and the toilet was still full with the overflow of water from the slough. As I opened the door of the outhouse, I suddenly knew how I could go and he would stay home. Inside the toilet were two holes, one for adults, one for children. I put him on the adult one, gave him a mighty push and down he went with a splash. I came to my senses then, realizing what I had done. He was screaming at the top of his lungs and as I couldn't pull him up, Dad had to fish him out.

While Mom washed him at the well Dad looked at me and asked, "You pushed him in?" My father has blue eyes that turn to ice when he's angry. It was impossible to lie so I said "Yes." He took a long green willow switch, peeled it and whipped my legs. When that one broke he took another until he had used four and my legs were swollen. I was sent to bed and Robbie was cleaned up and taken to the ball game.

Since that time I never did anything to either Jamie or Robbie, physically anyway. Instead I watched what Dad taught them and would practise by myself

33

until I had perfected whatever it was. Reward came whenever Daddy would say, "Dammit you boys! Maria can do it and she's a girl! Can't you do it at least half as good? If you can't, I'll send you in with the old ladies and get her to help me!"

Summer was always a great time because during those months Dad was home from trapping and could spend most of his time with us. In early June Mom would bake and pack food in the grub box while he would grease the wagon wheels and fit the harness. Then we would leave our house early in the morning and head for the bush to pick seneca root and berries. Our parents sat on the front seat of the wagon, Cheechum and Grannie Campbell and the littlest ones in the middle, Jamie, Robbie and I on top of the grub box, tent, or tailgate. Our four or five dogs and two goats ran behind and away we went.

By dinner-time three or four wagons of Halfbreeds had joined us along the way and everyone was talking and yelling and joking, excited at seeing one another and at the prospects of what lay ahead. By the time we pitched our tents for the night there were ten or more families in a long caravan. What a sight we must have been, each family with one or two grannies, grandpas, anywhere from six to fifteen children, four or five dogs, and horses trimmed with bells!

The evenings were great. The women cooked while the men pitched the tents and we kids ran about, shouting and fighting, tripping over dogs that barked and circled around us. Parents called to each other and slapped at their young ones, but only halfheartedly, because they too were enjoying themselves. We all sat down to supper outside and ate moose meat, ducks or whatever the men had killed that day, bannock baked on hot coals, with lard and tea, and all the boiled berries we could eat.

Afterwards we helped to clean up and for the rest of the daylight hours the men would wrestle, twist wrists, have target practice or play cards. Someone always had a fiddle and guitar and there was dancing and singing and visiting. We kids played bears and *witecoos* (a white monster who eats children at night) until it was too dark and we were called in to bed. Inside the tent were our blankets all spread on fragrant spruce boughs, freshly cut. A coal-oil lamp on the grub box gave some light. When we were put to bed the grown-ups would gather outside and an old grandpa or grannie would tell a story while someone built up the fire. Soon everyone was taking turns telling stories, and one by one we would creep out to sit in the background and listen.

Halfbreeds are very superstitious people. They believe in ghosts, spirits and any other kind of spook. Alex Vandal was the craziest, wildest man in our area and he believed with his heart and soul in the devil. He would tell about the time he came home from playing poker for three nights. His wife and ten children were asleep in the shack and it was fairly dark. His wife's sewing machine was beside the bed and as he came in, the little drawer in the bottom opened and a devil, the size of his hand, stepped out and jumped to the floor. Alex said he froze in terror. As it landed on the floor, it got bigger and bigger until it was taller than him. The eyes were red like fire and the tail switched. It smiled and said to Alex, "I helped you win the games, Alex, now I've come for your soul." Alex came to his senses and pulled out his rosary and held it in front of the devil who then disappeared.

And so the stories would go. The owls hooted and we would draw closer to our parents and grannies and they would hold us. Someone would again build the fire up until finally we all went to bed, paralyzed with fear. Then after lying quietly for a few minutes we would have to go to the toilet. Dad and Mom would never take us out, so our grannies would have to. I remember being so frightened that I couldn't pee

35

for the longest time, and I nearly fainted whenever a dog howled or branches moved in the wind. Soon the camp would be quiet, the silence broken once in a while by a mother crooning to her baby, awakened perhaps by the howl of a coyote or a wolf.

Some nights there was lots of excitement, like the time a bear crawled into John McAdams' tent and stepped on his wife! She shrieked and her children started screaming and they woke everyone in camp. The bear in his fright stood up and knocked the tent pole and the tent came tumbling down. All the men were trying to get the tent up, McAdams were crawling out from all over and the poor bear was trapped and growling with rage. Dogs were going crazy and everyone was yelling and talking at once. Needless to say everything was restored to order and we had bear "burgers" for dinner the next day. "Burger" is the right description because the bear was completely chopped up with axes, those being the handiest weapons for the men.

We worked like beavers during the daytime. Grown-ups would compete to see whose family picked the most roots or berries and parents would drive the children like slaves, yelling insults to each other all the while. Come supper-time and everyone would gather around while the old people weighed it all to see who had picked the most.

We had bad times during those trips too. For as much as we all looked forward to going to town, we knew our fathers would get drunk. The day would come when we had enough seneca roots and berries to sell, so we would all get bathed, load the wagons and go. The townspeople would stand on the sidewalks and hurl insults at us. Some would say, "Halfbreeds are in town, hide your valuables." If we walked into stores the white women and their children would leave and the storekeepers' wives, sons and daughters would watch that we didn't steal anything. I noticed a change in my parents' and other adults' attitudes.

They were happy and proud until we drove into town, then everyone became quiet and looked different. The men walked in front, looking straight ahead, their wives behind, and, I can never forget this, they had their heads down and never looked up. We kids trailed behind with our grannies in much the same manner.

When I first noticed this, I asked Momma why we had to walk as though we had done something bad and she answered, "Never mind, you'll understand when you're older." But I made up my mind then and there that I would never walk like them; I would walk tall and straight and I told my brothers and sisters to do the same. Cheechum heard me, and laying her hand on my head she said, "Never forget that, my girl. You always walk with your head up and if anyone says something then put out your chin and hold it higher."

Those days in town were both nightmare and fun, the evenings ugly yet at times humourous. After the roots and berries were sold, Daddy would give some money to Mom, some to our grannies and twenty-five cents to each of us and we went shopping. Mom and the grannies always bought flour, lard and tea, and then they would look for satin and silk material to make blouses, embroidery thread in all colours, and scarves. We kids bought comics and black licorice pipes. The men went to the beer parlour, promising to be out in half an hour.

After our shopping was done we all walked over to the wagons. We waited and waited until finally Mom and some of the braver women drove to the outskirts of town, set up tents and made a meal. Those times were quiet with little laughter or talk. Bedtime came with the warning that if Mom called us we were to run outside and hide.

Sure enough, about one or two in the morning the men returned, yelling and singing. Sometimes they were not too drunk but often they brought wine and started drinking outside the tents. Then Mom would call us and we would crawl out back of the tent, to hide in the bushes and watch until they all fell asleep. The men would get happy-drunk at first and as the evening progressed white men would come by. They all danced and sang together, then all too soon one of the white men would bother the women. Our men would become angry, but instead of fighting the white men they beat their wives. They ripped clothes off the women, hit them with fists or whips, knocked them down and kicked them until they were senseless.

When that was over, they fought each other in the same way. Meanwhile the white men stood together in a group, laughing and drinking, sometimes dragging a woman away. How I hated them! They were always gone when the sun came up. Our men would be sick and hung over and ugly-mean, the mothers black and blue and swollen. The men would go into the beer parlour every day until the money ran out and every evening the fighting would start again. After two or three days, we all left, usually at the request of the R.C.M.P.

One day we were visited by a committee of indignant townspeople, among them an Indian dressed in a suit, who told us to leave, but we were still waiting for our men so we stayed. We were very frightened, though the women tried to quieten us. One wagon was set on fire before we were left alone. Our men came back shortly afterwards and for once sobered up at the destruction they saw. They caught the horses and we were gone before dawn. I remember feeling guilty about the trouble we'd caused, and angry at myself for feeling apologetic.

Our summers were spent in this way until I was thirteen and those trips to town always became more unbearable, because little by little the women started to drink as well.

Chapter 5

There was an annual Trappers Convention in northern Saskatchewan every summer which Daddy attended faithfully. He would come home and be up half the night telling us what had happened. I remember crying each year because I wanted to go with him, for no particular reason except it was usually held in Prince Albert, and a city meant all sorts of exciting things to a little girl.

One day he came home and said that we could all go with him. I was getting ready for bed after the excitement of packing when Daddy told me to be sure and take all our fishing gear. Pack fishing gear to go to a city? I couldn't sleep, so finally I had to ask him where we were going to fish. He answered, "Montreal Lake, that's where we're going this year." I felt terribly let down. Who wanted to go to Montreal Lake where there was nothing but dogs and Indians?

However, next morning the prospects of such a long trip by car were just too exciting for an eight-year-old to waste time in pouting. Daddy had hired the storekeeper's son, Laroque, to drive us there. The car was a Model T convertible without a top, but I couldn't imagine going to the Convention in grander or more dashing style. The trip was to take us three days so we were really loaded down. Daddy, the driver and Jamie sat in front, Mom, Cheechum and I in the back with the tent, grub box, camping equipment and some traps. The traps were to be left in a cache somewhere by the road so that Daddy would not have to pack them in when he went trapping that fall.

We must have looked hilarious in that old red and green car with me perched on top of the load. The sun shone and what could be seen of the countryside was beautiful. The first thirty miles were so dusty that soon Mom put a handkerchief over her nose and mouth. The wind whipped at Cheechum's hair and she choked from the dust. She covered herself with a shawl and blasted Dad for wanting to travel like a white man.

We spent the first night with friends at Waskesiu, which was filled with tourists at that time of the year. Daddy said that some of them were "Long Knives" (Americans). We stopped at a restaurant for Mom to buy some ice cream. She got as far as the door and came back, looking as if she had seen something awful. Dad went in and came out with the ice cream, grinning from ear to ear. He wanted Grannie to see something special, so we waited a few minutes while Mom spoke angrily to him in Cree. I was nearly falling off my perch with curiosity to see what was inside when two white-haired ladies came out. They were both wearing two-piece bathing suits. One was quite fat and the other was well built and falling out all over.

Cheechum covered her face saying, *"Ayee ee. Tan-sa ay se yat chich o- kik."* ("What's wrong with these women?") Mom looked straight ahead. One of the women came over and asked if she could take a picture of us. They wanted a picture of Cheechum too, but she would not uncover her head, so they left, laughing and talking. Cheechum hit Laroque hard on the back with her cane to get him going, and as the car lurched forward I lost my ice cream. Normally I would have complained until my ice cream was replaced, but I was too astounded by the sight of those almost naked women who dared to walk among people and not be shy. That was my first impression of American women.

The road from Waskesiu was very bad, more like a wagon trail through muskeg and sand. There were rough stretches of corduroy—poles laid side by side across the road to keep travellers from sinking into the muskeg. It started to rain when we were half way there and we got stuck so many times that we lost count. We arrived late, soaked to the bone and dirty.

I will never forget my first sight of Montreal Lake. It was the biggest lake I had ever seen, dark and stormy-looking even though the sun was shining. It was dotted with islands and the shore had stretches of sandy and rocky beaches with miles of dense pine, tamarack and spruce. I had heard many stories of this lake from old trappers and Indians who had visited our home. I knew it had a monster fish that the Indians had seen many times over the years, and that many people had been drowned in storms and never found. Also, in the middle of this lake my Grandpa Campbell had seen lightning strike dead a man who had robbed the Sundance tree. There is nothing unusual about being struck by lightning except that in this case it happened in the middle of January.

The log houses were small, mostly one-roomed, and they seemed to blend in with their surroundings. There was a little whitewashed R.C. church and a Hudson's Bay store and various other buildings. There were children everywhere, and with the children were packs of grey and black dogs, big, husky animals, some of which were tied up, looking vicious and hungry. Daddy said that these people never used horses, they used dogs for everything. The smell was unbelievable. Every single thing smelled of fish, even the people. Their sole diet was fish, smoked or boiled, bannock and tea. The dogs, too, ate fish. The yards were littered with fish bones and heads. Everywhere there were little fires with racks over them where fish were spread to dry and smoke. These fires were tended by grannies like Cheechum with failing sight and no teeth. Working with them were little girls of my age who carried the wood and kept the dogs away.

Cheechum and Jamie and I went for a walk while camp was being set up and it was not long before Cheechum had made herself comfortable in front of one of the fires and had started visiting with an old lady. Jamie and I sat down on a log to listen and to eat a piece of smoked fish. When Cheechum finished her tea the old lady offered her a snuff box. She declined, but the little girl who was tending the firewood took a pinch and offered us some. We were too surprised to say anything so Cheechum said, "No they don't chew." That little girl could spit snuff dead on wherever she aimed, so I tried to copy her; but it was impossible for me to develop a taste for it.

The old ladies and little girls did all the work in the village. They did the cleaning and cooking, looked after the babies and mended the fish nets. The other women seemed to do nothing but sit around and talk or gamble. The little boys raced and played while the older boys and the men sat in groups and talked, or gambled, or slept.

We walked past one group seated on blankets, playing poker. Another group were playing the "hand game." This is a form of gambling with many variations, accompanied by Indian singing and drums. The players sit in two rows, facing each other, with a blanket between them. They have little bones under the blanket and the opposing sides have to guess which hand they are in.

Cheechum told me that we used to live in much the same way before the white people came. She said it was the job of the old women and little girls to tend to the housework and the fires. The older women were good trappers and hunters, better in some cases than the men. They went out on the traplines and helped their men in all the work. Boys never did much until they were older.

The women really impressed me for they were so free, although Mom with her convent background felt that they were quite shameless. They wore long bright skirts and blouses of satin in reds, blues and purples. Their long hair was oiled and braided with many barrettes, gay pins and ribbons, and the jewellery on their necks and arms jangled as they walked. I thought they were gorgeous, and the fact that many of them were blue-eyed made me feel that I had finally found my kin.

Blue eyes were unusual where I came from and we were teased by our brown- and black-eyed relatives. Cheechum said that these people were descendants of the first Hudson's Bay Scots to come to our North, and that despite the fact that they were treaty Indian they were more Halfbreed than we were—probably spawns of the Campbells, Simpsons and McLaughlins. As a child I believed that any Indian unfortunate enough to have blue eyes must have the devil Scot in him or her, and I would think, "There goes another spawn of Satan." I was very disappointed when the first Scot I met was brown-eyed, short and meek-looking instead of the legendary figure I envisioned—a bearded giant with wild hair and blazing blue eyes.

When we arrived back at our camp to change and clean up, Cheechum made me hurry as we had been invited out for supper. She oiled her hair with bear grease and braided it, then oiled and neatly braided mine as well. She put on her best purple blouse, black skirt and shawl, and away we went. We must have reeked of bear fat, but I guess we were in style for when we reached the house everyone crowded around to kiss us and shake our hands. The home was very small with a packed dirt floor and a fireplace made of clay or mud and willow sticks. There was a table but we all ate outside. I loved fish and ate until I burst. An old man sitting across from me was eating so quickly that it was hard to keep up with him, and as fast as he ate the bones flew out of the side of his mouth. We visited there until late at night, then watched the people pow-wow until almost morning.

The Convention officially started that day, but I have only one memory of it. Two men were trying to out-shout Daddy who was very angry about the trapline boundaries. They were almost ready to fight when the meeting was brought to order. The man who had the most to say against Daddy was sitting in front of Cheechum. When the meeting started again, Dad brought up his point once more and again the man jumped up and started yelling. Cheechum took a safety pin from her blouse, stretched it open and when the man sat down she pushed it into his backside. The poor man jumped to his feet and started to say something, but with one look at Cheechum he sat down and never said another word for the rest of the afternoon.

There was one thing that was special about Montreal Lake and that was the medicine. I had often heard the old people talk about Montreal Lake and the strength of the people there. I listened to these stories and asked Cheechum to explain what I did not understand. Many native people practised medicine, but Montreal Lake was renowned for its bad medicine. The men used it on their traplines so they would have good hauls. They would also go onto other people's lines and take their fur. No one dared to fight back. They could cast spells and even kill with it. They used it on each other sometimes, after fights, and they could catch any man or woman they wanted with special love spells.

When we arrived at Montreal Lake I knew about the medicine, but was too young to care about it. However, little as I was, I felt it as soon as we got there. It is hard to describe or explain as it is something you cannot see or hear, only feel and smell. It is so frightening at first that your hair almost stands up on end, then the effect levels out and while you remain aware of it all the time, it is not so intense.

The smell is unlike anything else: heavy and musky and almost human. Sometimes it's almost overpowering, and then suddenly it's gone like it was not even there. The night of the pow wow I saw a woman under a love spell. She was about Mom's age and very pretty. She was with an older man and followed him everywhere, never taking her eyes off him. She had a husband and children but acted as if she didn't know them or see them. There was one woman whose face looked as though someone had grabbed her and twisted the skin and eyes. She had taken someone's husband and the wife had put a spell on her. One man was unable to walk because someone had used bad medicine on his trapline and caused him to lose the use of his legs. He almost froze to death but managed to crawl back to his camp.

I became curious and wanted to talk to different people, but Cheechum warned me severely against it. Cheechum and Dad always impressed upon us this one thing: never ever fool around with anyone who uses medicine. If someone used medicine on you, you had to find a more powerful medicine man or woman to either remove or return the spell.

Whenever Grannie Dubuque planned to visit us we became excited as we anticipated the boxes of goodies, clothing, bedding and toys that we knew would come with her. But we seldom saw her as she lived in Prince Albert. She cleaned for well-to-do families in Prince Albert and the things she brought were all cast-offs given to her by employers.

Momma would tell us to mind our manners and to take care not to ruin our good clothes, which we always wore while Grannie was there. Daddy never said much during these visits. He would become quiet, and he and Cheechum would often leave for a

few days. Grannie always arrived in style, usually in
an old Model T Ford that she hired in town. She wore
nice silk dresses trimmed with white lace and a white
lacey handkerchief tucked into her belt. She also wore
a small hat with a veil, gloves, and shoes with heels
while carrying a real handbag. She was the only
woman I remember in my childhood who used face
powder and perfume. She would hug and kiss Momma
and the children, inspecting us carefully. Once settled
in the house she watched while we tore through the
boxes and tried on the wonderful assortment of
clothes. Then came our presents, usually dolls, china
dishes, trucks and trains. Momma would receive a
special gift, maybe a new dress or shoes. But most of
all I remember the pretzels. Being the oldest and her
favourite, she would give a huge box of them to me
which I shared with the others.

Grannie generally stayed for a week and in that
time our lives changed. We used a tablecloth and ate
bread instead of bannock. Momma took special pains
in cooking the game and somehow we managed to
have cakes with our wild fruit preserves. Cheechum,
who grudgingly came back after the excitement died
down, looked on disapprovingly but said nothing. I
would be really spoiled by the time Grannie left and,
as Daddy said, impossible to live with until straightened out with the help of a willow switch.

The year I was seven Grannie Dubuque brought
a different kind of gift for her special granddaughter.
At dinner, after her arrival, she announced a surprise.
She had made arrangements for me to go to a residential school in Beauval. It sounded exciting, but looking
at Dad's shocked face, Mom's happy one, and Cheechum's stony expression—a sure sign of anger—I was
confused. Dad went out after dinner and did not return until the next day. Meanwhile Momma and Grannie planned my wardrobe. I remember only the ugly
black stockings, woolly and very itchy, and the little
red tam I had to wear and how much I hated it.

I can recall little from that part of my life besides feeling lonely and frightened when I was left with the Sister at the school. The place smelled unpleasantly of soap and old women, and I could hear my footsteps echoing through the building. We prayed endlessly, but I cannot recall ever doing much reading or schoolwork as Momma had said I would—just the prayers and my job, which was cleaning the dorms and hallways. I do recall most vividly a punishment I once received. We weren't allowed to speak Cree, only French and English, and for disobeying this, I was pushed into a small closet with no windows or light, and locked in for what seemed like hours. I was almost paralyzed with fright when they came to let me out. I remember the last day of school, and the sense of freedom I felt when Dad came for me. He promised that I would never have to go back, as a school was being built at home.

Chapter 6

The school was built in Spring River when I was nine. It was three miles away, and on opening all the parents had to bring their children for registration. Because it was a mixed school, whites and Halfbreeds were gathered together officially for the first time, but the whites sat down on one side of the room while the Halfbreeds sat on the other. We were also to be inoculated. We didn't know this of course because the teacher felt that if she told our parents we might not come. So there we were, all scrubbed and shining, our fathers and mothers looking proudly on.

The teacher called the roll and parents were to stand in front of her and answer questions. Alex Vandal, the village joker, was at his best that day. He had told Daddy that he was going to act retarded because the whites thought we were anyway, so when his son's name was called he shuffled over. The teacher asked for the first name. Alex replied, "Boy." Then he looked dumbly around and finally yelled at his wife in French and Cree. "Oh, the name is Paul." The teacher then asked whether Paul knew his ABC's? "No." "Does he count?" "No." "Does he know his prayers?" "No." "Does your son believe in Jesus Christ?" "No." "Don't you believe in Jesus?" "I don't know, I never saw the god." Our people looked straight ahead trying not to laugh and the whites were tittering. Alex and Paul returned to their seats all smiles.

When registration was finished, the nurse came in

and told the parents what she had to do. She began on our side first, but we didn't realize what was happening until we saw her stick a needle in my brother's arm. Then we started screaming and crying. The parents became excited as well. Dad had to hold me while I kicked and fought with all my might. Then the needle went in and Daddy fainted dead away. We arrived home late in the afternoon, a bedraggled bunch, everyone sniffling and red-eyed with sore arms—our parents completely exhausted. They laughed about it later and Daddy was teased for a long time.

School wasn't too bad—Heaven compared to the Residential School. We had a lot of fights with the white kids, but finally, after beating them soundly, we were left alone. There were many remarks made but we learned to ignore or accept them as time went on. Daddy was concerned with the distance we had to go to school, so one day he came home with a mule. What a horrible, ugly animal, especially when we had our hearts set on a good saddle horse! Dad made a saddle for us and in spite of my pleas we had to climb on one morning and start for school. We went a few yards and the mule stopped. Dad hit it and petted it, but nothing worked, so finally we got off and walked, happy that we did not have to disgrace ourselves by riding that old thing. Our happiness was short-lived however. When we came home, my aunt Ellen, Daddy's youngest sister, was riding Mule around the yard at a good clip. She was leaning over, dangling a pole with grass tied to it in front of his nose. Naturally he was never able to catch it, but he certainly tried. And that's how we went to school during that fall and part of the winter. In January it got too cold for us to hold the pole, and Mule, getting smart, started to balk again. Dad finally sold him and we got our horse, not the beautiful, graceful animal of our dreams, but an old quiet Clydesdale mare. Each day we stopped for three cousins, and all five of us rode Nelly to school. We had her until she was unable to move without discomfort from old age, and Dad put her out of her misery.

We Halfbreeds always played by ourselves unless there was rugby or a ball game, when we played against the whites. It was the same in class; we stayed in two separate groups. Lunch hours were really rough when we started school because we had not realized, until then, the difference in our diets. They had white or brown bread, boiled eggs, apples, cakes, cookies, and jars of milk. We were lucky to have these even at Christmas. We took bannock for lunch, spread with lard and filled with wild meat, and if there was no meat we had cold potatoes and salt and pepper, or else whole roasted gophers with sage dressing. No apples or fruit, but if we were lucky there was a jam sandwich for dessert. The first few days the whites were speechless when they saw Alex's children with gophers and the rest of us trading a sandwich, a leg, or dressing. They would tease and call, "Gophers, gophers, Road Allowance people eat gophers." We fought back of course but we were terribly hurt and above all ashamed. I remember coming home and saying ugly things to Mom. She took me in her arms and tried to hold me, but I kicked her and said that I hated her, Daddy, and "all of you no-good Halfbreeds." She turned away and went outside and a few minutes later Daddy came in and tried to talk to me. When I said the same things to him he just sat there while I cried and shouted that the other kids had oranges, apples, cakes, and nice clothes and that all we had were gophers, moose meat, ugly dresses and patchy pants. Cheechum was sitting on her pallet listening through all this and when Dad said nothing, she got up and led me outside. She didn't speak for the longest time, just walked. When we were about half a mile from the house she told me to get her a long willow stick and bring it to her. Then she told me to sit beside her and listen.

Many years ago, she said, when she was only a

little girl, the Halfbreeds came west. They left good homes behind in their search for a place where they could live as they wished. Later a leader arose from these people who said that if they worked hard and fought for what they believed in they would win against all odds. Despite the hardships, they gave all they had for this one desperate chance of being free, but because some of them said, "I want good clothes and horses and you no-good Halfbreeds are ruining it for me," they lost their dream. She continued: "They fought each other just as you are fighting your mother and father today. The white man saw that that was a more powerful weapon than anything else with which to beat the Halfbreeds, and he used it and still does today. Already they are using it on you. They try to make you hate your people." She stood up then and said, "I will beat you each time I hear you talk as you did. If you don't like what you have, then stop fighting your parents and do something about it yourself." With that, she beat me until my legs and arms were swollen with welts. After she was finished she sat with me till I had stopped crying, and then we walked home. Nothing more was ever said about clothes or food. My first real lesson had been learnt. I always tried to keep my head up and defend my friends and cousins in front of those white kids, even when I knew we were wrong. Sometimes it was very hard to control my disappointment and frustration, and many hours were spent with Cheechum telling her how I felt, and she in turn would try to make me understand.

A family of Seventh-Day Adventists lived a couple of miles from our house on the same road. Their two children, a boy and a girl, were very pale, sickly and timid-looking, but they acted very authoritarian and superior towards us. On the way home from school we often chased and tormented them. In the winter they drove to school in a small caboose warmed by a wood heater. A caboose is a square wooden box with a door at the back. It has runners

51

and a peephole in front to see and to put the reins through. We would hide by the side of the road and scare their old horse so badly it would run away, tipping over the caboose. It's a wonder they weren't burned alive. Next morning the teacher would receive a letter from the parents and we would be whipped in front of the class, but in the afternoon we would make it just as bad for them until they learned to shut up. After a while they decided it was safer to be on our side and so they tried to be friendly. They gave us their lunches as bribes. They could have had ours but they never did develop a taste for gophers or lard.

Our first teacher was a sad-looking little Englishwoman in her late forties. She had never taught Halfbreeds before and we soon realized that she didn't like us. I remember her long straight skirts, her black woven stockings and ugly black shoes. She had very little hair, and what little she had she scraped back into a bun. She loved to sing and her favourite song was "O Canada." I can still see her whenever I hear that song, waving her arms up and down, completely off key and getting all red in the face from the effort. We had many different teachers during those years; some got the girls pregnant and had to leave; others were alcoholic; and because our school attracted everybody else's rejects, we had a constant stream of teachers. We had one good teacher, Mrs. Park, who was stern but fair. Maybe it was because she treated us as equals that I liked her and did well in school.

When I started school my hair was waist-length and so curly it was almost impossible to comb without pain for me and frustration for Mom. She wanted to cut it but Dad forbade her and threatened anyone who even mentioned scissors and Maria in one breath. Mom combed my hair and wrapped it around her fingers to make long, fat ringlets that fell down around my shoulders. She liked to put a bow on top, and that was even worse than the combing. I knew it looked ridiculous because I was always in short pants, boys' shirts and bare feet. With warts on my hands and with such dark skin, I knew that ringlets and me did not belong together. Poor Momma, she wanted to have a feminine little girl so badly.

My hair was one of Cheechum's pet grievances and she would attack it with the same patience and determination that she revealed whenever she decided to change something. It was fine with me whenever she braided my hair since I wouldn't have to comb it as often. She would spend an hour rubbing bear grease into it and then braid it. The grease was to keep the curls from popping out of the braids and to give me a shiny, tidy look.

My hair, so thick and so full of bear grease, was a perfect place for head lice, and I was deloused at least twice a month. We never had lice at home but some of the kids with whom I played had them. Daddy laughed while Momma sighed, as she washed my hair in coal oil, muttering all the while about Cheechum whom she knew would rub in the bear grease again. Cheechum would say, "Just wait my girl, your Cheechum will make your hair straight yet." And today at thirty-three, my hair is straight as a poker.

Our days were spent at school, the evenings doing our chores. Daddy was away trapping from early October until Christmas, and again during the beaver season in spring. How we missed him! It was as if part of us was gone with him, and we were not complete until he had returned. I remember the times he came home, always on Christmas Eve. The food supply in our settlement would be very low at that time of year as the men were all gone on the traplines. However Grannie Campbell and my aunts would bring food they had been saving for a long time to our house. They steamed a pudding, which was called a "son of a bitch in a sack," made of raisins, flour, baking powder, sugar and spices. They made cakes with frosty icing, sprinkled with coloured sugar, and baked blue-

berry, cranberry and saskatoon pies. The smells would
be heavenly, because at that time of year our sole diet
was wild meat and potatoes. There was no bannock as
the flour was being saved for the holiday baking. On
Christmas Eve, Grannie, Mom, Jamie and I always
went into the bush for a tree. We decorated it with
red and green crêpe paper, some ornaments Mom had
from her mother, and strings of pop corn coloured
with crêpe paper. There was an angel for the top
branch, but no one put it there for that was Daddy's
job. Then Mom laid out our best clothes while we all
bathed in a washtub, and then put us to bed. At ten-
thirty we got up and dressed for midnight Mass. It
was a thrilling time—outside we could hear sleigh
bells ringing and people laughing and calling back
and forth as they drove to church.

Right in the middle of all this Daddy would always walk in, with a full-grown beard and a sack full
of fur on his back. First he swung Mom off her feet
and kissed her, and then we climbed all over him. I
remember that he always smelled like wild mink. He
washed himself while Mom and Grannie put his packs
away, then we all dressed warmly and walked to
church with Grannie Campbell. Cheechum stayed
home and kept the fire going.

After Mass we talked around the big heater in the
church, and friends and relatives all kissed each other.
Then we'd all go home, for that was the one night
families spent together at home. Daddy would tell us
all the things that had happened to him while he was
on the trapline. While Mom tidied up and my grannies
smoked their pipes, he put the angel on the tree, and
we would say our prayers and go to bed.

Jamie and I always woke everyone up at five o'-
clock. In the living room our stockings were plumb
full and overflowing with nuts and candy canes, oranges and apples—the only ones we ate all year. Under the tree there were gifts for everyone. Mom got a
comb and mirror from Daddy; he got shaving lotion;

and our grannies got cloth for new dresses. We were given blocks made and painted by Dad and Mom, home-made dolls which looked like the modern day "Raggedy Anns," and shoes from our grannies. Then Daddy made pancakes. That was the only meal he ever cooked while Mom was still alive. He made huge pancakes, and while we all stood around, wide-eyed and breathless, he would toss them in the air and catch them right back in the pan.

Christmas dinner was the highlight of the day. It consisted of meat balls rolled in flour, stewed moose meat, all covered with moose fat, mashed potatoes, gravy, baked squash and pemmican made of dried meat ground to a powder and mixed with raisins, smashed chokecherries and sugar. After that we filled ourselves with the pudding and cakes until we could hardly move.

All the families visited back and forth during the holidays. After supper, furniture was moved against the wall or put outside while the fiddlers tuned their fiddles. Soon they were sawing out a mean hoedown or a Red River jig, and everyone was dancing. Each family held a dance each evening and we never missed any of them. The hostess baked a nickel inside her cake and whoever got it in his piece held the dance the next night. We stuffed ourselves during those holidays until we hurt, because it would be a year before we would eat like that again. One thing about our people is that they never hoard. If they have something they share all of it with each other, regardless of good or bad fortune. Maybe that's why we're so damn poor.

Old Yes-Sant Arcand put on a dance at his house once a year and invited everyone. He lived on top of a very steep hill with a lake at the bottom. His grandchildren used the hill for a slide in winter and poured water down it so that it was really icy, and with a sled you could go almost to the middle of the lake. I remember one party he had in particular. We all came—

Campbells and Vandals together from our area, as well as Arcands from the other area and the Sandy Lake Indians too. As we arrived Mom said, "There's going to be a fight for sure with those Sandy Lake people here," but I paid little attention because there was never a good dance unless there was a good fight. Yes-Sant's cabin was a very long one-room log house with a big stove and heater, and four beds on one side. He had dragged all the furniture outside so there was plenty of room to dance. He was also the proud owner of the largest cellar in the country with a huge trapdoor on the floor.

Everybody was enjoying themselves, dancing and eating, when suddenly a fight broke out. The mothers chased all the little kids under the beds and we big ones climbed up to the beams to watch. Soon everyone was fighting and no one knew who was hitting who—Dad even punched out his brother. The heater pipes were knocked over and there was smoke everywhere; then the kitchen stove pipes went down. Dad finally made it to the door and threw it open. Whenever someone came near the door Daddy would slug him and he would go sliding head first or backwards down the slippery hill to the lake. The lights went out and it was pitch black inside, mothers were yelling, kids screaming—a total mass of confusion! Cheechum got Mom and another lady to help her open the trapdoor and some of the men fell in. Finally, everyone was either down the hill or in the cellar. (When they tried to climb out Cheechum would hit them on the head with her cane.) When everything had settled down, the women lit the lamps and laughed as they set the place to order and got us kids back to bed. Cheechum shut the trapdoor and said, "Let them all stay in the cellar and by the time the others climb the hill they'll all be sober." So furniture was hauled back in while some women made tea and everyone sat down to laugh and eat. The men outside weren't able to climb the hill, so they went into the barn with the

horses to keep warm. When daylight came they found
the path leading up to the house. Cheechum scolded
them well and then she opened the trapdoor and let
the others out. What a sight they were with black eyes
and smashed noses, nearly frozen and feeling foolish!
She scolded them too, and hit a few. We never had a
dance without a good fight and we enjoyed and
looked forward to it as much as the dancing.

Next to the Christmas festivities, our people looked
forward to weddings. Weddings were something special, and were gay and gala affairs, in which everyone
in our area and other communities participated. Flow-
ers were made from bright crêpe paper; yards and
yards of decorations were made for the houses and the
horses. The best-matched team was used for the bride
and groom, with a bright red cutter in winter and a
red buggie in summer. The horses would have their
manes and tails braided the previous day, then they
would be brushed and curried until their coats shone
and their manes and tails hung in waves. The harness
was oiled and strung with bells, and from a long wire
hung braided coloured ribbons that fluttered as the
horses pranced.

Everyone lined up in the procession with their
horses decorated as well. The bride wore a white satin
dress which had been worn by many other brides and
was altered so many times you could see all the different stitches. The bottom of the dress was trimmed
with rows and rows of bright satin ribbons and on the
bride's head was a long veil made from cheese cloth,
with a halo of little crêpe paper rosettes. The groom
was dressed in dark pants and a white or blue satin
shirt embroidered with bright floral designs. He wore
a band on his arm trimmed with bright ribbons. The
horses never galloped or ran—they must have known it
was a special occasion as they would arch their heads
and prance and dance all the way to church. After the
ceremony we would all go to the biggest house in the

community where the women would have the food all ready. For two days there would be feasting and dancing and laughter.

The bride and groom would then move into their new home built by the men in the community. On their first night together the rest of us would collect pans, whistles, drums, anything—and sneak over. Then we would all yell and scream and bang the pots and pans together till the couple would both come out and make a speech. We loved weddings and our women could hardly wait until they were rested up from one to start match-making again.

Chapter 7

Daddy used to hunt a lot when he was home. The meat would be brought back to the house, cut up and hidden. He sold it to farmers around us and as far away as Prince Albert. This extra money supplemented our budget and helped to keep us going until the next time he had fur to sell. The game wardens and the RCMP were constant visitors at our home and they searched all around our house and yard and in the homes of my aunts, uncles and Grannie Campbell. Daddy hunted in the National Park which was illegal and was often almost caught. I remember times when someone would ride to our house, the horse all lathered up, and warn us that the game wardens were coming. Daddy and Mom would grab the meat and run outside to hide it, usually in the church basement. (The priest found it once, and after that Daddy had to give him some whenever he wanted it.) Meanwhile Cheechum would throw all the bloody items in the stove and build a fire. By the time the wardens arrived Daddy would be sleeping and Mom and Cheechum drinking tea. Of course we were repeatedly cautioned never to tell anyone, even our best friends, because it was illegal for Halfbreeds to have game out of season, and it was a greater sin to get it in the Park. Usually we ran away when we saw them coming, but one winter day, Joe Vandal rode over to warn us and helped us to hide everything. Daddy had a hole dug on the side of the hill where he made his whiskey in summer. It was like a big cellar closed by a trapdoor, covered with earth that had little spruce trees growing on it. Inside he had three elk hides and one moose, plus three to four hundred pounds of meat. I went with him to make sure it was closed properly, and he told us to slide our sleigh over the door and make tracks so it would look like a play area. And that's where we were playing when the wardens and Mounties arrived in two Bombardiers.

Instead of going to the house as usual, two of them came over to us. One warden started talking to us, but didn't get any information as we were too shy and afraid. While he was speaking, the Mountie took some candy bars out of his pocket and held one out. When I reached for it he said, "Where does your Daddy keep his meat, Honey?" I sold out for an "Oh Henry!" chocolate bar. I led him right over to the trapdoor, showed him how to open it, and while eating the candy, even told him about the church basement and how Daddy had to give that mean old priest meat. I then took the men to the house. I will remember forever the look on Mom's face and the way Dad laughed when I walked in with chocolate all over my face and said, "Here's my Dad." They were drinking tea at the table. Mom jumped up and said in Cree, "You wicked girl!" and made a grab for me, but Dad stopped her. He looked at me and started to smile. Then he laughed and laughed. Cheechum was slamming pots around and Mom just sat there, staring at me. It was only then that I realized what I had done. The Mountie put handcuffs on Dad while I screamed and cried and beat at him, telling him he had fooled me. Dad kissed me before he left and said not to cry, that he was not angry. The wardens took all the meat and hides plus the whiskey still. I did not see Daddy for six months. He was in jail in Prince Albert. I received many scoldings that winter from Mom and I did extra work the whole time.

It was a hard six months for all of us. We had no

money and no meat. I had to set rabbit snares every day, and Mom and I would take the .22 and shoot partridges, ducks and whatever we could get. Mom was a terrible hunter but Daddy had trained me well. I didn't mind the hard work, in fact I felt I should be horsewhipped for what I had done. We had to charge our groceries at the store and our credit was limited. Dad still laughs about it but I have hated chocolate bars ever since, nor have I ever trusted wardens and Mounties.

The Law will do many things to see that justice is done. Your poverty, your family, the circumstances, none of it matters. The important thing is that a man broke a law. He has a choice, and shouldn't break that law again. Instead, he can go on relief and become a living shell, to be scorned and ridiculed even more. One of my teachers once read from St. Matthew, Chapter 5, Verses 3 to 12: "Blessed are the poor in spirit for they shall inherit the Kingdom of Heaven." Our class discussed this, using Native people as examples. I became very angry and said, "Big deal. So us poor Halfbreeds and Indians are to inherit the Kingdom of Heaven, but not till we're dead. Keep it!" My teacher was furious and looking at me said, "Verse 13: 'Ye are the salt of the Earth but if the salt have lost his savour wherewith shall it be salted? It is thenceforth good for nothing, but to be cast out and to be trodden underfoot of men.'" Then she closed the book and I had to kneel in the corner holding up the Bible for the rest of the afternoon. It was her favourite punishment. My arms would be sore but I dared not let that Bible fall, for her wrath was worse than Sodom and Gomorrah. I used to believe there was no worse sin in this country than to be poor.

One afternoon, a couple of wagonloads of people arrived, driven by one of Mom's uncles, Jeremy, who weighed over three hundred pounds, and a friend, Chi Pierre, who was very small. They brought their wives and twenty-one children as they were out of grub and came to Dad so that he could feed their families and take them hunting. Although I was pretty young I had gone on many hunting trips with Dad, so he took me with him on his horse. Elk were calling when we arrived at dark in the National Park and made our way to our usual camping place. Suddenly Dad motioned for everyone to stop, but Jeremy and Chi Pierre were arguing loudly in French, Cree and English and didn't hear him. Dad jumped off his horse, threw me beside a tree and told me not to move. I looked up in time to see a huge bull elk heading straight for us. He looked twice as big and black in the dark and he was mad. Dad fired a shot and I could feel the elk rush by me toward Jeremy and Chi Pierre, and then fall. He was snorting and bellowing. Dad ran past, yelling for the two men to get out of the way. However, they were nowhere to be seen. Our horses were running away. The elk was stumbling and trying to get up. Suddenly I heard loud voices and as I reached Daddy he started to laugh and pointed to a scrubby tree in front of us. At the very top was Jeremy and he was shaking the tree and yelling in Cree and French, "Get off, it's my tree." Chi Pierre, who was trying to climb the tree, kept sliding down and cursed in the same mixture of languages, "I'm your brother-in-law. He'll kill me." The elk was under the tree, bellowing and falling down and getting up. Dad shot it again, then he pulled me down beside him and laughed and listened to them. Finally Jeremy's branch broke and he fell off. He landed on the elk and Chi Pierre climbed to the top. Poor Jeremy, he was in a state of panic and didn't realize the elk was dead. Dad and I were laughing so hard we couldn't talk. When Jeremy finally realized the elk was dead and saw us, he picked himself up, brushed off his pants and said, "Ye Christe my Nees-tow, we almost had trouble here." It was one of the funniest hunting trips I was ever on.

I remember another elk we raised practically

from birth. He would come into the house until his horns grew so big that Mom refused to let him inside anymore. We called him Bannock because he loved bannock so much. Poor Bannock would go mad when he knew we were eating and he couldn't come in and join us any more, so Daddy made the window bigger and he would hang his head inside and be with us. Then one day he left and we didn't see him for over two years.

Daddy was out in the barn one afternoon when he heard Mom screaming, so he raced to the house. A huge elk was trying to get inside. We were all crying from fright as there were two more elk directly behind it. Daddy saw us all and started to laugh. When he finally recovered himself, he opened the window and the elk put his head through. Sure enough it was Bannock. Wild animals are funny and smart—like Bannock returning and bringing his friends, almost as though he'd said, "Come along, panhandling is good here." Bannock and his friends stayed for a couple of weeks but then some hunters shot them.

Sometimes in the evening when people were visiting, we children listened to them tell ghost stories, and because we lived beside the cemetery those stories would keep us awake long into the night. Daddy always seemed to run out of tobacco about eight o'clock in the evening and Jamie or I would have to go to the store. To get there we had to take a foot path down the hill, climb a barbed-wire fence into the graveyard, walk between rows of graves, climb over another fence, and go around the blacksmith shop to the store. We knew every single person buried in that graveyard for we had listened to so many stories about each one.

One grave in particular, right beside the fence, had a horrible story associated with it. Grannie Campbell used to tell us that the old man buried in it was called "Ke-qua-hawk-as," which means wolverine in Cree. He was just as mean and as ugly as the animal, and never allowed anyone near his house, not even relatives. They all died before he did and because there was no family left, the Halfbreeds got together to build his coffin. They held a wake for him at Grannie's house. The men didn't finish digging his grave until quite late. Old Mrs. Vandal was outside, alone, when she heard someone talking. She listened and it was coming from the empty grave. The spirit of Wolverine was standing there complaining about the size of his grave and how useless those people were. So Mrs. Vandal got very angry and told him he should be happy that someone was kind enough to make him a grave after having always been so miserable. The men found her beside the hole shaking her fist. Grannie said every so often on certain nights you could still hear Wolverine complaining.

Whenever I had to go to the store in the evening I would jump the fence and run as fast as I could, feeling sure that Wolverine was behind me. I would jump the other fence and arrive at the store completely out of breath. And then going home through that graveyard again I would nearly die. It was worse climbing the hill as I couldn't see behind me. Daddy's youngest brother, Robert, was a terrible tease and was never afraid of ghosts. He would lie beside old Wolverine's grave and when I came back from the store he would make scratching noises and talk in low gruff tones. I would be stiff with fright and would walk by the grave looking straight ahead. As I climbed over the fence he would groan louder and scratch harder. I would pee my pants from fear while running up the hill, and he would pound the ground to make a sound like footsteps right behind me. When I burst into the house babbling and screaming, Daddy would go out and see nothing. This happened several times and one night I couldn't stand any more. I came through the graveyard and heard those noises again, the groaning and scratching, and as I climbed the fence there was

64

an awful scream and noises like someone falling and running towards me. I crumpled down and fainted.

I came to, at home, with Mom rubbing my wrists. Uncle Robert sat in a corner with a most terrified look on his face, all scratched up and bloody. He said that he was coming from the store behind me and Wolverine grabbed him and knocked him down, bawled him out for using his graveyard and chased him away. He was too frightened to go home alone, so when Daddy came back he went with him. After Dad returned he laughed until he cried, then told us what had happened. He had followed Robert to the graveyard one night and watched him scare me, so this night he asked Mom to send me to the store again while he went ahead and hid in the bushes behind the grave. Then, when Robert came sneaking down, he waited until I had gone by. Robert was so absorbed in making his noises he heard nothing. Daddy had on an old fur coat and hat and he grabbed Robert's arm and groaned in his face. Poor Robert nearly died. He screamed and started to run, so Daddy grabbed his feet and when he fell, climbed on his back and berated him for sitting on his grave. He said he would haunt him forever if he came near again. Poor Uncle, he finally got away and raced to the hill, but forgot the barbed-wire fence and ran right into it. He picked himself up, and ran past me, racing to our house. Mom came and found me and carried me home. I had no more trouble with Wolverine after that, but I was still frightened of that graveyard. In a way I liked being afraid, and if Jamie had to go to the store instead of me I was disappointed.

Like many other kids, I ran away from home. Once Mom had a sheet of writing paper, and because money was so scarce the paper was precious. When I asked for it and was refused, I stole it. Caught by Daddy and given a good licking, I sat up in my tree and planned to run away. I was eight years old then. I would go to St. Michele, a small village nearby, which was like a city to me, get a job and make lots of money. Then I would buy a new car, a red satin dress and red shoes, and I would drive by the house, toot the horn and everyone would come out. I would not speak to them and they would all be sorry. So down the tree I climbed, went home to pack my clothes in a grape basket, and sneaked out. This was about ten o'clock in the morning. By noon I reached the river, where I met Robert (my idol and secret sweetheart) riding to our place to visit my aunt. I told him I was leaving home and said good-bye. He laughed and rode on. By four o'clock I was starving and scared and wanted to go home, so I turned back. Arriving at the river after dark, I saw lanterns and people everywhere. Some were calling me, so I crawled behind a boulder and listened. I heard Uncle Robert say he had found my scarf by the river and that Daddy thought I had fallen in and drowned. I crept off and ran the rest of the way home crying. When I got there, I saw wagons and people all around so I crawled in a window and found Jamie crying in bed. He promptly hugged and kissed me and said everyone was sure I had been drowned and Daddy and all the men were looking for my body. We heard Mom and Grannie crying, and then the men came back and said they were going for the RCMP to drag the river. Everyone was crying so Jamie and I started to cry too. We went back to bed and talked about what would happen when they had a funeral for me. I became so upset when Jamie said I would have to lie beside Wolverine I couldn't stand it any longer. I burst into the kitchen, yelling that I didn't want to be buried beside Wolverine, and scared all those people half to death. Mom grabbed me and hugged me and cried, and so did all the women. Dad gave me a licking and a half, and said that if I ever ran away again he would see to it that I became Wolverine's partner.

When someone died, the funeral wake was held at our house because we were beside the church and grave-yard. The body would be brought in and the women would wash and dress it. The men would build the coffin and dig the grave. Everyone had to help in-cluding us kids. When the coffin was completed it would be covered with black broadcloth with crosses made of white satin ribbon on the top and sides. We all wore black arm bands. The wake would last three days. The women cooked lots of food and then we sat around the body all day and night saying rosaries ev-ery hour. As each person arrived he was given some-thing to keep from a pile of articles owned by the de-ceased. Then Mass would be held and the body buried.

Our funerals were never like the funerals here, where everyone cries and carries on, or goes into a state of shock. We grieved, but in a different way. The women cried, but they accepted death, and when it came, met it with great strength and kept their grief inside as they did with so many other things. Funerals were like weddings as far as seeing old friends and relatives was concerned. People would come from miles and miles away to visit.

The pallbearers wore suits and it was the only time in my life that I ever saw my father or any of our men in suits. There were six in our whole country and the owners were very special people whom we chil-dren regarded with awe. To own a suit and hat was a real status symbol. Of course we always believed that they were only for funerals, just like black broadcloth and white satin ribbon and waxed crêpe paper flow-ers. When I look at the old pictures of funerals now, I have to laugh. Two of the owners were small men, three were really tall, and one was really skinny with a big belly. The suits were dark blue and black with stripes and wide lapels, old and out of style even when I was little.

,The pallbearers' pants were halfway up their legs and their sleeves far too short or too long, jackets too big or so tight the wearer would have to be careful. No one had a big belly so that one pair of pants was always bunched up with a belt and held up with suspenders which we called braces. They looked grand to me then, but now it is funny and sad. It was the only thing no one made jokes about. As far as everyone was concerned the suits were holy.

I was never afraid of those bodies at our house, because I helped Momma with the preparations. However, I remember one time when I was really scared. Daddy had gone trapping, when Gene was killed, at a fight after a party in St. Michele. Someone found him the next morning, and instead of reporting it, a burial was held and we had no wake for fear the Mounties would come. A few months later someone told the RCMP. They came with doctors to dig up the body and examined it at an abandoned house. Everyone was worried and meetings were held all over so that our stories would be straight. Because Dad had been absent he was called upon to identify the body and help with the investigation.

Jamie and I were dying of curiosity and as no one would say anything in front of us, we decided to investigate. The house had sheets over the windows and a Mountie stationed at the door. We sneaked behind the house and climbed through a hole in the roof and looked down. The body was on a table, naked, with the head over the edge. Gene's hair was hanging to the floor. He had had short hair when he was buried. A doctor was sawing the top of his head off and we felt so sick that we climbed down and raced home and jumped into bed. That evening when Daddy came home he had to go to bed too. Two young constables were left behind to put the body back in the grave. It was getting dark, so they came to get Daddy to help. When they were lowering the body the rope slipped and the cover fell off the casket and jarred the

bandages off the head. One Mountie started to go
down to fix it but was afraid. They asked Dad to do it
while they held the lantern. So he went down, but as
he straightened the bandage, his hand slipped and he
touched the brain. He quickly threw the lid on the
coffin and climbed out. For weeks we all had night-
mares and no one ever went near the house. Someone
finally burned it. The case came up in court but no
evidence could be given. The Halfbreeds needed in-
terpreters so if an English-French interpreter was
called they would say that they talked only Cree and
when a Cree speaker was brought in it was vice versa.
By the time the stories were translated, they were so
mixed up that the case was closed.

Chapter 8

The CCF party was in power in Saskatchewan for a long time. I remember our people got into some good fights over it. Some things stand out in my memory. A member of the provincial legislature lived down the road from us. When he ran in the election he promised our people relief work for which they would be paid.

One of the projects was clearing land for a huge pasture. There was very little money for fancy equipment but plenty of manpower—the Halfbreeds from the MLA's riding. He told everyone who wanted jobs that a truck would pick them up at the store on a certain Monday. Daddy and I drove over by buggy that day to see them. When we arrived the men were in harness like horses, pulling up stumps and trees. Dad started to laugh when he saw Alex Vandal coming towards us pulling a tree, sweating and panting. He looked at us and said, "Danny, did you know the new government felt sorry for us because we're called 'Halfbreeds'? They passed a law changing our name and now we're CCF horses. The Americans are going to pay good money to come and look at us." All the CCF horses soon quit, and that was one CCF tourist attraction that went broke!

This same man used to come to our house, and once in a while he caught my Mom frying meat. We weren't afraid as he was one of Daddy's better customers for both meat and homemade whiskey. Both he and his wife were drinkers and would go off for

two or three days, leaving their kids to run the farm.
Mom never approved of them but Dad got along well
with him. However, after he won the election, he and
his wife changed and became very active in the Bap-
tist church. He painted his old car bright blue and
started wearing suits.

One day he drove up and Dad invited him in for
something to eat and a drink. He said no, he didn't
care for a drink or food, and then gave Dad a lecture
about the evils of alcohol and poaching. Cheechum
was worried when he left and urged us to hide the
meat and whiskey.

The following morning the wardens and the
Mounties came. They turned the place upside down
and found nothing. Daddy was furious, so on Saturday night he went over to the store where the in-
former was giving a speech to a group of people. He
walked over and kicked the box out from under him
and gave him the beating of his life. No one tried to
stop him as they all felt it was deserved. When the
next election was called the MLA lost his seat, and he
and his wife went back to drinking Campbell whiskey
and eating the King's game.

Another man whom I remember, not as a politi-
cian but as a lawyer, was John Diefenbaker from
Prince Albert. He was not just a lawyer to us, as that
did not mean much, he was also colourful, dashing
and exciting and he would represent anyone, rich or
poor, red or white. If they had a case and had no
money he would help. If John was representing someone we knew, our people would come for miles in rain
or snow to watch him. Then they would go home and
repeat what had happened, and by the second repeti-
tion John was ten feet taller.

He helped us, and the important thing was that
he did so when no one else would. And he did it with
the style and colour my people loved. Cheechum
never said anything good about him but she never
said anything bad either.

My people have always been very political. They get involved in political campaigns for local white politicians. As a child I remember listening to them talk and argue far into the night about why this party or that was the best. They talked about better education, a better way of life, but mostly about land for our people. However, when one of our own people said to hell with white politicians—let's get our own men in, or organize our own people into a strong association—that was something else. Uncle Miles used to say often that we had to do it ourselves, because no one would do it for us, and then he'd explain why, but no one really listened until Jim Brady and Malcolm Morris came to our country.

They were from Alberta and they told our people how the Halfbreeds in Alberta had organized an association and had gotten colony lands through one united voice. We could do it here too, if we organized a strong body and elected a man to speak for us. Daddy started going to the meetings to listen to these men. He became a strong supporter of Jim Brady and he spent hours and days talking to our people, and taking them to meetings. Everyone was excited. The government was finally going to give the Halfbreeds land.

Cheechum was excited for the first time and would pace the floor until Daddy got home from his meetings and tell Mom and Cheechum and Grannie all that had happened. Grannie Campbell was against what Daddy was getting involved in and tried to get him to stay home and forget about the meetings. She told Daddy he would only get hurt, the government wouldn't give us anything, and he'd probably end up in jail for his trouble. Cheechum would get angry and tell her to leave Daddy alone. She said it was his duty as head of our family to do what had to be done, that we'd never get past our mud shacks if he just sat and waited. Even if nothing happened and he did go to jail, he at least tried, and he could give his children no greater gift.

How proud I was of my Dad! I wanted to help but all I could do was brush and curry Daddy's horse so that it would look good when he rode to the meetings. Then one night Dad said we could go with him. We arrived about eight-thirty and I followed Daddy around and listened while the men visited and talked about what was happening. I grew tingly all over with excitement. The meeting finally started with Miles Isbister as the chairman and Jim Brady as the speaker. Jim said almost word for word what I have heard our leaders discuss today: the poverty, the death of trapping as our livelihood, the education of our children, the loss of land, and the attitude of both governments towards our plight. He talked about a strong united voice that would demand justice for our people—an organization that government couldn't ignore. He said many people were poor, not just us, and maybe someday we could put all our differences aside and walk together and build a better country for all our children.

After the meeting was over, people visited and talked some more. Daddy brought Jim over and introduced him to us. He started to say something to Mom, but before he finished I told him I thought he was wonderful and that Cheechum had already told me all the things he'd said. When I saw all the grownups looking at me I hid my face in Cheechum's apron. He reached down and gave me a hug and from that night on Jim Brady was my hero and I loved him as I loved no man but my Dad.

On the way home I lay in the back of the wagon with my head on Cheechum's knee and while she stroked my hair I thought of all I'd heard that night. Cheechum had told me that someday a man like Jim Brady would come, and she said when he came many more would follow. I felt something new inside me. It was an emotion that is hard to describe—almost like happiness, pride and hurt all at once. The feeling was all knotted up in my guts and made me feel very lonely for something I couldn't see or understand. That night was the first time the feeling ever came; it was a feeling I was to get often in my life.

Daddy went to meetings all that year. He didn't go trapping and so we were very poor. He was gone nearly all the time, and when he was home he would be very moody, either so happy that he was singing, or else very quiet. We all suffered these times with him. It seemed that the Mounties and wardens were always at our house now. We were treated badly at school, even our teacher would make jokes about Dad, like, "Saskatchewan has a new Riel. Campbells have quit poaching to take up the new rebellion." That year I think I fought every white kid in that school and then failed my grade besides. Some of our relatives wouldn't visit or talk to us. Like the whites, they laughed and made jokes about Dad. The whites didn't matter; I could accept their ridicule, but our own people I could not understand. Cheechum talked to me and tried to make me realize why people did this. She would tell me, "Ignore them, they are nothing, only frightened people. They laugh with the whites because it is the first time in their lives that the white man has talked to them like men." It was so true. For the first time I saw whites inviting Halfbreeds to their homes. Some days I saw them riding home together in cars, laughing and drinking like brothers. I hated those men! How could they be so fooled!

Soon people were saying that Daddy didn't trap because he was getting paid by Communists, and more people turned against us. We never saw money and lived on gophers and bannock nearly all the time. Our home life also changed, and often I heard Momma crying. Only Cheechum did not change; she encouraged Dad and did all she could to help him. Momma loved Daddy but could not take what was being said about him. She begged him to quit. Then one night, he did just that. Something inside him died, and he became another defeated man.

One night I was awake waiting for him to come home from a meeting. Mom and Cheechum were sitting at the table sewing. As soon as I heard his step I ran to the bedroom door so I could listen. Daddy's shoulders were all stooped; he looked like an old man. He sat down and put his head on the table and began to cry. It was the first time I'd ever heard my father cry. Mom put her arms around him and held him, while Cheechum just sat there and said nothing. Finally Daddy said to her, "Grannie, we've failed. We can't do it." I crept back to bed and later, when I heard Cheechum go outside, I followed her. We said nothing for a long time—just sat there beside the slough and listened to the frogs sing. Finally Cheechum put her arms around me, and holding me close, said, "It will come, my girl, someday it will come." She told me then that some of the men had been hired by government, and that this had caused much fighting among our people, and had divided them.

Daddy started to drink that summer and I began to grow up. Our whole lives, and those of our people, started to go downhill. We had always been poor, but we'd had love and laughter and warmth to share with each other. We didn't have even that anymore, and we were poorer than ever. Daddy still trapped, but only because it was an escape for him. He would be gone for long periods at a time, then when he was home he drank and often brought white men home with him. Sometimes he'd hit Mom, and she would take the baby and run away until he was sober. He seldom smiled and he hardly ever talked to us unless it was to yell. When he sobered up he'd try to make up, but it never lasted long. Once he even slapped Cheechum.

We never saw any of the men again who had come to lead our people. They had found government jobs and didn't have time for us anymore. Jim Brady went far into the north and I never saw him again either.

Grannie Campbell was dying of cancer that summer and when she asked for Dad no one could find him. He came home the day before the funeral and for months after he would cry and call her name when he was drunk. Have you ever watched a man die inside? Children who have grow up fast. Jamie and Robbie and I had to take over the responsibility of helping to raise our family. There were seven children, even though Momma lost three babies in three years. We cut pickets and dragged them to the store, as many as twenty at a time, and sold them for five cents a post. We cut pulpwood, peeled it, and when we had enough we hired a man and wagon to take it to the store. We got eight or ten dollars for each load. We set snares for rabbits and sold the fur for five cents each and ate the meat. Gopher's tails were a penny apiece. Jamie and I would go to the store for flour and lard and stand at the counter longing for the things on display. I was full of bitterness over what had happened that year and was angry at my father, but above all I hated the men who had fought him. I told Mom that he was no better for quitting than the Breeds who laughed at him, that he did not have to give up and start drinking. But she just told me to love Daddy, that he would come out of it and soon everything would be all right; as for him quitting, if he had listened to Grannie Campbell this would never have happened, that it was all useless and the only way we would get ahead was to forget about the meetings and just do our best each day. I felt that in a way she too betrayed Dad by not understanding what he had to do. Her concerns were for her family. She didn't realize that what happened outside was important too.

Cheechum listened to me when I told her how I felt, and cursed our men for being weak. She would tell me, "Wait my girl. It will come. I've waited for

ninety years and listened to many men. I have seen
men quit and have felt as you do, but we have to keep
waiting and as each man stands unafraid we have to
believe he is the one and encourage him. You'll feel
discouraged like this many times in your life but, like
me, you'll wait."

Mom was often sick through that year and spent
three months in hospital after an operation on her
throat. She became pregnant shortly afterwards and
was ill most of the time she carried that baby. Dad
finally realized that what he was doing was not only
destroying himself but his family as well. He quit his
drinking and tried to pick up where he had left off,
but it was never the same again.

I had bad dreams for six months before Momma
went to the hospital to have the baby. Often I woke
up screaming for her not to go. I would dream that
she was making a coat for herself from one of Uncle
Frank's old army overcoats. She would finish it and
then take the shiny buttons to sew them on. She
would start from the bottom and when she had sewn
on the sixth and last button she would die and leave
us alone. Then one day I came home from school and
Mom was sewing that coat. I tried to tell her, but she
said it was only a dream—that I was too full of ghost
stories and superstitions and should forget that non-
sense. So I told Cheechum and she tried to stop her
also.

Momma went to the hospital early in the morning
of May the first. Daddy borrowed a buggy and they
went as far as St. Michele and took the train to Prince
Albert. I knew that day I would never see her again.
She kissed us all good-bye, climbed into the buggy,
fastened the last button on that coat, and they drove
away. Cheechum and I cried, and when we were
alone she told me that now I had become a woman. I
would be responsible for the little ones and for
Daddy. She said she would stay and help me but that
she was getting old and could do little work. She held

me for a long time. That night I put the younger ones
to bed and we said our prayers like Momma always
told us to do. Cheechum and I waited for Daddy to
come home with news. The frogs were singing and
while she and I drank tea we listened to them. I was
so empty that night, not lonely, just empty. I fell
asleep shortly after midnight but woke when Daddy
drove in. He came and knelt down beside me and
said, "Maria, you are the oldest one and now you have
to help me. Momma died this afternoon." He put his
head on my knee and held me. We just stayed there
for a long time.

My aunts and uncles and friends started to arrive.
All the grown-ups were crying and the little ones
woke up. I went into the bedroom and gathered them
around me and told them. Only Jamie and Robbie understood, so I asked them to help me put the little
ones to bed again. When the youngest were asleep, we
three went outside. We walked and walked and finally
sat down and cried. Cheechum found us and took us
in. Mom's body was brought home for the wake and
for the first time in her life she had something brand
new—a coffin all done in black and silver. When the
casket was opened, I was horrified. Momma had on lipstick and rouge and her hair was curled. Cheechum
asked everyone to leave the two of us alone. When they
had left the room, we washed Momma's face, braided
her hair and wrapped it around her head the way she
had worn it for years.

Funeral services were to be held in the Roman
Catholic church. On the day of the funeral, Father
Cardinal came over and told Daddy that he would not
hold services for Mom because Daddy had not called
a priest in to administer the Last Sacrament before
she died. We could, however, bury her in the cemetery. Daddy said nothing. Momma's death had been
so sudden he hadn't thought of calling in a priest. My
uncle left then and came back with an Anglican minister from the nearby Reserve. Father Cardinal stood

at the door of the church the whole time the service was being held and made sure no one tried to ring the bells for her. While she lived Momma never missed church and many times the last of our money went to the collection rather than to buy food. She always said, "Hush, it's for God." But the bells could not even ring for her funeral. For years after, I felt as if it were my fault—that Father had refused to give Momma a Mass because of all the torment I'd caused him.

Chapter 9

Everything seemed to go wrong after Momma left us.
We never realized before what a pillar of strength she
was, and how she had kept our lives running
smoothly. There was very little money around. Fur
was poor, which meant that trapping was finished. All
the rocks and roots had been picked in nearby settlements. All our people were having hard times and had
nothing to share with us or each other. Relief was
unheard of then, unless for the crippled or aged. Dad
was in a world of his own and we rarely saw him for
the first few months after Mom's death. He would dis-
appear for days or weeks on end. I don't know what
I would have done during that time if it had not been
for Cheechum. She gave me strength to carry on my
work—I was only twelve and with Momma gone and
Dad away, I had to take over not only as mother but
father as well. Jamie worked that summer for the first
time; he was eleven years old. He did summer fallow
and general farm chores for a farmer who lived near
us. For this he was paid sixty dollars a month plus his
room and board, which was a fortune to us. He was
up at four-thirty and worked until ten o'clock at night.
And because the farmer was a Seventh-Day Adventist,
Jamie had to work on Sunday instead of Saturday, but
it didn't matter because we didn't go to church any
more.

   Dad came home one day after having been gone
for a long time, and Cheechum talked to him for

hours. He seemed to realize then that Momma really was gone and he had to do something about us, or the relief people would come and we would be gone too. He changed after that, but we still had a difficult time; I get tired just thinking of those years.

How hard it must have been for him! He had to mother us, love us, feed and clothe us besides working. In spite of the problems Dad and Momma had before Momma died, they were very close and always shared in everything. Now he had only Cheechum to talk to. Many times after we had all gone to bed, I heard Dad cry and call for Momma in his sleep. Cheechum would wake him and talk with him far into the night. I started to fail in my studies at school because I spent so much time worrying about what was happening at home. I often begged Daddy to let me quit school, but he would tell me that I needed education and that it was the most important thing in my life.

Daddy spent a great deal of time with us that year. In the evenings we read to him just as we did when Mom was alive, or talked or just cuddled up to him. This was also the time for mending or whatever else had to be done. Then at nine o'clock we would kneel together and say our rosary. I resented the Church and God during this half hour, and hated every minute of it, but felt I could endure it if it made Dad feel better. He told me a long time afterwards that Mom had made him promise we would pray before bedtime, and after a while he found that those prayers comforted him and helped him to carry on; that it was not the Church he was praying to but to God.

Dad is still deeply religious in his own way, but I have never found peace in a church or in prayer. Perhaps Cheechum had a lot to do with that. Her philosophy was much more practical, soothing and exciting, and in her way I found comfort. She told me not to worry about the Devil, or where God lived, or what would happen after death. She said that regardless of how hard I might pray or how many hours I spent on my knees, I had no choice in what would happen to me or when I would die. She said it was a pure waste of time that could be used more constructively.

She taught me to see beauty in all things around me; that inside each thing a spirit lived, that it was vital too, regardless of whether it was only a leaf or a blade of grass, and by recognizing its life and beauty I was accepting God. She said that each time I did something it was a prayer, regardless of whether it was good or bad; that heaven and hell were man-made and here on earth; that there was no death, only that the body becomes old from life on earth and that the soul must be reborn, because it is young; that when my body became old my spirit would leave and I'd come back and live again. She said God lives in you and looks like you, and not to worry about him floating around in a beard and white cloak; that the Devil lives in you and all things, and that he looks like you and not like a cow. She often shook her head at the pictures I gave her of God, angels and devils and the things they did. She laughed when she saw the picture of the Devil turning people over with a fork in the depth of Hell's fire, and remarked that it was no wonder those people looked so unhappy, if that's what they believed in. Her explanation made much more sense than anything Christianity had ever taught me.

Mom had had a baby in the hospital, a little boy. No one even thought of him at all during the funeral and the next couple of weeks. In fact, I didn't even know we had a baby until the nurse brought it home. I assumed it had died too. So there we were. I was twelve years old, Jamie was eleven, Robby eight, Dolores six, Peggie four, Edward three, Danny one and a half, and we were presented with a brand new baby who had just got out of an incubator. Cheechum and Dad were away that day so we were at home alone when the nurse came with him. She told us what to feed him and left. We had no cows for milk and no money to buy any. Poor Geordie had cried himself to sleep from hunger by the time Dad and Cheechum got home. Dad sent us to a nearby farm for milk and I made arrangements to get it twice a day, wondering all the time how we would have twenty cents a day to pay for it. Then came the job of finding clothes, diapers, bottles and so on. An aunt made the clothes and we used an old beer bottle with a nipple, and when he was ready to eat solid foods, he had whatever we had, all mashed up.

Dad found a job with a farmer for the summer and fall, and with Jamie and him both working we managed to survive our first year. We planted a huge garden of potatoes, turnips, carrots and cabbages. Although the soil was very poor, we managed to get a good crop of vegetables. I took all the kids berry picking, then under Cheechum's directions, canned over two hundred quarts that first fall. I made jars and jars of pickles while Robbie cleaned our dugout basement and built bins for storing the vegetables. Besides all the gardening and canning, I had to bake, cook, wash clothes twice a week on a scrub-board, make enough lye soap to last us for six months, unravel old tattered socks, sweaters and mitts to knit new ones. Dad brought home sacks of raw wool that had to be washed, carded and made into yarn, all by hand. There were old clothes to mend and the old coats to be remade for everyone. I was so tired sometimes that I would tell Cheechum, "I just can't do it anymore." She would reply, "You have to. Once you learn to do it right it will be easier." I don't know how I ever managed to do it all before school started in September.

School was about to start and we had not even discussed what we would do with the small ones. Cheechum was too old to chase after them outside. She could get along well in the house, but the two little boys were just too much for her; they were always wandering off into the bush and we had to be quick to find them.

And so our first housekeeper arrived. She was in her twenties, utterly lazy and irresponsible. She wanted sixty dollars a month, yet felt she could stay in bed till noon each day. She liked children but didn't look after them, so when Danny got lost for nearly a day Daddy fired her. A whole succession of housekeepers followed during that first year. Then one night we heard Daddy say to Cheechum that he would just have to remarry. My God, what a panic we were in! We didn't want a stepmother and didn't think it was right for him to remarry. All housekeepers thus became potential stepmothers and therefore the enemy, and we made sure that they never wanted us for a family.

One afternoon Cheechum told us that she was leaving because she was too old to be anything but a burden to us. She was ninety-six that year. She packed her things and her nephew came for her the next day. How completely alone I felt! I had been so close to her all those years, constantly at her side, and although she said that I would see her often, it was even harder than losing Momma. We became poorer and poorer, if that was possible. We never received assistance, for Dad was afraid that if we received help they would visit our house all the time. I guess in his own way he was too proud. So our lives continued until our teacher reported us to the relief people and they said there was going to be an investigation into our situation. That night Dad told us we would be moving in a few days.

Chapter 10

Dad had a job twenty-five miles away with a farmer he had known for years. The man offered us a house half a mile from his own plus a hundred and twenty-five dollars a month, and all the milk we could use if we did our own milking. There was a school nearby, just across a hollow.

We arrived at our new home late in the afternoon, all nine of us and our belongings piled in the wagon. We had left nearly all our furniture behind as there was no room to take it with us. Dad said he would get it some day soon, but that day never came. I remember Dad locking the door of the home he had built for his family. The house looked so lonely; it looked the way we felt.

The kids were excited and happy with their new surroundings. There was a slough nearby and lots of bush, so they had plenty of things to keep them interested and busy. Jamie and I unpacked our few things and tried to clean that barn of a house, which seemed so desolate and unfriendly compared to our comfortable log home. The only consolation was that the relief man would not find us and we could be together.

I was scrubbing floors and Jamie was putting dishes in the cupboards when he said, "Maria, it will even be easier for us to go to school here—if our babysitters are no good we can run home and check up." I started to cry at that point, but we ended by laughing as I always felt foolish for being so weak.

Our new place was a big frame house with a kitchen and pantry, living room and bedroom on the main floor, and two bedrooms upstairs. It looked bare because we had nothing to put inside it. In the kitchen there was an old square table which Daddy rebuilt to accommodate all of us, a couple of benches, a cupboard, an old wood stove which never worked properly, an old washstand and wood box. The living room had nothing except Dad's rocking chair. He made beds for all of us with old boards, and we had our mattresses from home filled with fresh straw.

Dad ploughed a big garden for me and I organized the little ones to weed and hoe. They picked berries too, and by fall I had filled every one of three hundred jars bought at an auction sale. When the berries and vegetables were finished, I canned moose meat. It was packed into jars, salted, and then boiled for three hours in the washtub.

We finally got settled down and Dad started work. Jamie found a job as well, doing chores and mending fences, and I started to prepare again for school and winter. I had a long hard talk with myself and made up my mind that I was going to do the best I could here, regardless of what happened. It was our chance to get ahead and I even day-dreamed that I would make it through high school, and that we would all make good friends and become part of the community. But it didn't work out like that.

One warm, sunny day Dad and Jamie were working and we were home alone. Robbie had drowned a couple of gophers and we decided to cook them outside. He built a fire while I skinned and gutted the gophers. Then we put them on sticks pushed into the ground and bent over the fire. I put some bannock in a frying pan to bake, and Edward, the third youngest, decided that he wanted to roast the intestines while everyone was waiting. They are really delicious, roasted and salted. I cleaned them out and the little ones were holding them over the fire when Dad's boss

and son drove into the yard. I will never forget how
they looked when they saw what we were cooking. I
knew that by supper time all the neighbours would
know that we ate gophers, so when Mr. Grey asked if
that was all we had to eat, I lied. They shook their
heads and laughed and drove away. We had no meat
or vegetables then, as our garden was not yet ready
and Daddy had no time to hunt while he was working.

We got a housekeeper that fall, a young Indian
girl who was able to get along with and manage the
little ones fairly well. School began in September and
for the first time everyone had new jeans, shirts and
shoes, sent by Grannie Dubuque. She had been too ill
after Momma's death to help us in any way.

School was heaven to me, at first, because I could
be young for a few hours each day. I could forget the
cooking and cleaning at home and there was time to
read. I read everything I could find and thought
about the big cities I had read about with good food
and beautiful clothes, where there was no poverty and
everyone was happy. I would go to these cities someday and lead a gay, rich, exciting life.

Our teacher was a young woman from a good,
middle-class Christian family. She was ambitious and
wanted to have a large farm and fine house, but her
husband liked to drink, dance and run around. She
had different moods—sometimes she was very prim
and proper, and sometimes just the opposite, and I realize now that these were often caused by personal
problems.

We were the first Halfbreeds she had taught and
although she tried to hide her prejudices, she was often cruel. Then she would feel guilty about her out-
bursts and overwhelm us with kindness. During class
she would often ridicule us for mistakes. Peggie was
in the first grade, a very small six year old, timid and
shy. Because we used a mixture of Cree and English
at home, her pronunciation was poor. The teacher

would shake her and say to the class, "Look at her! She is so stupid she can't even say 'this', instead of 'dis.'" She would make Peggie stand up at the front of the room for an hour, without moving. She grew so afraid of school that she would cry and wet her bed at night.

During a ten minute health program in the mornings, one of the pupils had to check everyone for clean hands and neck, brushed teeth and so on. The student called out our names and when she said "Maria Campbell," I stood up. "Did you brush your teeth?" We never brushed our teeth, but I answered "Yes." Robbie was always getting x's as his fingernails were never clean and his hands were chapped and dirty. One day, the teacher found his ears dirty again and told him that if he wasn't clean tomorrow, she would clean him up properly. Robbie washed well the next morning but forgot to do his ears. So she took him to the cloakroom and with a scrub brush—the kind you use on floors—started scrubbing his hands, neck and ears. We all sat still for a long time, waiting for her to finish. Soon I heard Robbie whimpering and became alarmed. He had always been a real toughie, and if he cried he was really hurt. I went into the cloakroom. She had him bent over the basin, his poor little neck was bleeding and so were his wrists. She was starting on his ears with the brush when I snatched it away and slapped her. We got into a fight and Jamie finally pulled me away and took us all home. I was so angry I would have killed her if I had found something to smash her head. Jamie went to get Daddy, as I was sure that we had all been expelled, while I put salve on Robbie's scrapes. Daddy came home accompanied by Mr. Grey, and when Dad saw Robbie he got very angry. Mr. Grey told him to quieten down and that he would call a Board meeting that night. The teacher never bothered us again, and in fact, tried her best to be nice. In time my brothers and sisters forgot and even liked her, but I never forgot or became friendly.

There was no work after harvest was finished, so Daddy decided to trap until Christmas as we were getting short of everything. He left us in November with enough food to last until his return, but we ran out of flour and staples early in December. It was really cold that year and we had more snow than usual. We knew that Daddy could not be home for two or three weeks, so we decided to go to the store at our old home, twenty-five miles away, where we could buy on credit. It was an icy, snowy day. Our housekeeper was afraid that we might freeze, but we assured her that we knew what we were doing. Jamie got the team ready and, with Robbie, put the hayrack on the sleigh so that we would have plenty of room. We loaded it up with an old armchair and mattresses, then put the little ones on the chair, with hot stones wrapped in blankets at their feet. We decided to go on an old trail across country as it was shorter than the main road. (I don't know what possessed us, for we certainly knew better.) About five miles from the house, the snow started to blow and we lost the trail. Soon the horses were up to their bellies in drifts and I knew we were lost.

The children were getting cold and started to cry. I realized what could happen to us and started to panic, but Jamie remained calm and told me not to be scared or the little ones would be frightened. He finally found a fence and followed it, leading the horses back to the road. We were lucky to get home with only frozen cheeks and fingers.

So, we had nothing to eat except canned meat and berries and a little flour. Christmas was coming and we could not even bake a cake. The blizzard lasted nearly a week and we were afraid for Daddy. We did not want to go to Mr. Grey, as he might call the relief people, so whenever he stopped to see us, we told him that we were getting along fine.

Robbie caught a very bad chest cold on that trip and it grew worse each day. Finally, his fever was so

high that he went completely out of his mind and
could hardly breathe. I remembered that Momma and
Cheechum used to make a broth from bark of green
poplar for colds, and that they boiled certain roots for
fever. Jamie went out and got me some bark and roots
and for three days we fed Robbie as much broth as he
could swallow. It was bitter stuff. We bathed him
with cool water and finally the fever broke; but it was
a while before he could get out of bed.

By now I was sure that we would never see
Daddy again. Our food was nearly all gone, the house
was drafty and cold, the younger kids were sick and
Christmas was only one day away. Jamie told me,
"We're going to get ready for Christmas because
Daddy will be home tonight. He always comes home
on Christmas Eve." He cut a tree and we decorated it
with pine cones as there was nothing else, not even
crêpe paper. The angel and the few ornaments which
belonged to Mom were set aside for Daddy to put up.
I was very depressed that whole day and evening, and
worried what to tell the little ones if Daddy didn't get
home. Jamie and I were still up, when shortly after
midnight, Daddy came walking in. He had bags of
groceries and big boxes of gifts. Later, when we were
in the kitchen having tea, he handed me a small bag.
Inside were two hundred and fifty dollars. He told me
to buy clothes for everyone after Christmas and whatever else was needed.

Christmas was a sad time, even if Daddy was
home. He tried to make us happy, but in spite of all
our efforts we were a lonely family. Our people were
too far away to visit and we missed the excitement
and love we shared at home with them. We sat down
and tried to eat Christmas dinner, but the roast beef
and new toys couldn't replace what we had known.
We had never eaten beef before and we found it flat
and flavourless. The new toys broke the first day; we
had always had hand-made gifts that lasted forever.

Poor Daddy, it seemed that the harder he tried, the rougher it all became.

Grannie Dubuque arrived during the holidays and we were so happy to see her. She expected us to be poor, but I don't think she expected what she saw. She cried as she kissed us all and because we were so starved for a woman's affection and love, we almost overwhelmed her.

Everything went back to its old order of peace and quiet. The little food we had tasted better, our endless sewing and mending seemed like fun; and above all, we older ones had someone who would put her arms around us and hold us close if we were hurt.

Grannie was kind and gentle like Mom but where Mom had been quiet, she was noisy and full of fun. She would cook our dinner, then tell us that we were having chicken-a-la-king—whatever that was—and we would set the table with an old sheet taken from a bed and pretend we were rich. We would taste all the fancy salads and dishes she'd prepared, though of course they were only meat, potatoes, bannock, lard and tea.

Grannie was a combination of a very strict Catholic and a superstitious Indian, which made her the greatest storyteller in the world. Every evening, after work was done, she made each of us a cup of cocoa and some popcorn, and then gathered us around her and told stories of the northern lights (ghost dancers), of Almighty Voice, Poundmaker and other famous Indians. We heard many spine-chilling tales, but we asked for one story in particular, over and over again.

It was about an only child whose parents were older people. The little girl was very spoiled and was forever whining and crying. She died of a sickness when she was only six years old. A couple of days after the burial her parents discovered her hand sticking out of the grave. They went to the priest who told them that this was their punishment for spoiling her, and that if they wanted the little girl to rest in peace and go to heaven they must take a switch and whip her hand as they should have done when she was living. So each day they did this until the hand was gone. In its place was a little rosary to show that the child had gone to heaven. We were always scared and spooked while Grannie told this story. One night a figure came crashing through the window behind her chair. Glass flew everywhere as we screamed and raced from the room with Grannie right behind us. Soon we heard moaning, and Jamie peeked in. Poor Robbie was sprawled on the floor, cut and bleeding. He had slipped away from the storytelling and was trying to sneak out from the upstairs window on a rope. Somehow his pants caught and when he kicked loose, he slid down the rope too fast and hit the window. What a fright he gave us! Grannie laughed until she cried as she washed him off and I put cardboard over the window.

Chapter 11

Dad left to go trapping again and we went back to school after the holidays while Grannie started housekeeping in earnest. Bob (the son of Mr. Grey, Dad's boss) and his wife Ellen lived only six miles away and often came to see us. They treated Jamie and me as equals and were probably the first good white people I knew. We often visited them too, spending the whole day riding, tobogganing or just talking and playing cards.

Ellen had a younger sister Karen, fourteen years old like me. Her father had died just a week before my Momma, so we found comfort in each other, and she spent a great deal of time at our house. She lived with her mother who taught in an all-Halfbreed school in another district. She didn't dislike me or other Native people, and was good to us so long as we kept in our place. My friendship with Karen, however, broke the unwritten law of each staying on his own side. Later when Jamie and Karen started to spend some time together, Karen's mother became very cold and rude and tried in many ways to break up our friendship.

Bob and Ellen moved to the farm when Mr. Grey retired to Prince Albert. Karen would stay at Ellen's for the weekend and be at our house the whole time. She had a Shetland pony and I had old Nellie, and we rode everywhere. When Ellen became pregnant and could no longer ride, she lent me her Welsh pony. We rode everywhere on those ponies, going on picnics and talking all the while. Karen was the first person I ever confided in, other than Cheechum. I told her about the hard time we were having, and how afraid we were of the relief people and the wardens and the Mounties. With Daddy hunting and trapping in the Park they were at our house constantly. She understood our fears and poverty and helped us when she could. We had many dreams, the two of us, but so different from each other's. She took her lovely home for granted and all the things they had, but admired the way we lived and preferred to be with us; my constant ambition was to finish school and take my family away to the city, giving them all Karen had and more.

While Grannie was with us for those few months, I had time to be just a fourteen-year-old girl and I started to notice boys for the first time.

No one had ever talked to me about life, babies or boys. Dad had often tried but would become very confused and put it off. Cheechum and Grannie must have taken for granted that Momma had talked to me. Most girls my age already knew everything, but I was completely ignorant. I came home from school one afternoon very frightened. Jamie and I were very close but Robbie was the only one I could talk to about personal matters, so I told him what was happening to me. He said, "Oh, don't worry about it. It's normal for girls to get like that. I heard the guys talking about it." I was so alarmed at the thought of having periods for the rest of my life that he went to find some older guys and learn all about it. Meanwhile I stayed in bed and certainly didn't have to pretend that I was sick. The cramps were so bad I was sure mushrooms I had eaten earlier must have poisoned me. Robbie came back a while later, carrying a box of Kotex, with the information that I would have periods a couple of days every month, unless I was going to have a baby. I was so relieved: I was not poisoned after all and this period thing would only last two days.

Karen and I both fell in love that summer, but our boyfriends didn't know we existed. The boy Karen liked was in my school and I tried everything to bring them together, without much success. I didn't work on mine at all, just suffered in silence as I felt I had no chance with anyone. I was almost five feet six and very thin. My hair was so short and curly it was almost impossible to comb. Instead of tanning a golden brown my already dark complexion would go almost black during the summer. Black hair was supposed to have, as the storybooks went, snapping black eyes or sparkling brown ones. Mine were green. My aunts, uncles and cousins all had brown or black eyes and used to tease me for having dark hair and skin—"like a nigger" they said—and eyes like a white man. The Indian kids made fun of me and called me names in Cree. The old people called me "owl eyes."

One day we met our "boyfriends" accidentally-on-purpose at the store. They rode along with us, and we stopped half-way home to talk. Just as we were leaving, Harold, the boy I was mad about, helped me on my horse and kissed the top of my head. I was thrilled to death. Harold was seventeen and six feet tall, a beautiful Swede who was the dream of every girl in the country. Already many mothers with marriageable daughters were inviting him to suppers and dinners. He was considered a good match because he was an only child who would inherit a good farm.

Karen and I came home in a daze. I was so happy I couldn't believe my luck. I didn't see him for nearly a week, and then I saw him at Ellen's with a girl from a nearby farm. He was standing by the door and tousled my hair as I went by. He introduced me to his girlfriend and said, "This is Maria. She's the girl I was telling Mom I'd love to have for a little sister. She can ride, hunt, shoot and do anything a grown guy can do. She's Dannie's daughter." I didn't stop to say hello but

95

raced upstairs. I was completely heart-broken and swore I would never have anything to do with men again. Mom had warned me that men liked dainty ladies, not girls who ran wild and dressed like boys.

I moped around for days and suddenly I remembered that I had not had my periods again. I became frantic, certain that I was going to have a baby. I told Karen and she wanted to tell Ellen, but I was frightened that Dad would find out. We talked it over and I told her that I would get rid of it. I often heard the old ladies talk about miscarriages and how to cause them. We told Jamie and Robbie and they were as frightened as we were. So we started "operation miscarriage."

Karen had heard her mother and another lady say once that the best method was to sit in a tub of hot water. Jamie and Robbie dragged the washtub into the bush, hauled water for it and built a fire. I sat in hot water for a whole day but nothing happened. Then I jumped over logs and rocks and rode horseback at full gallop. After three days of this, I finally decided to jump off the roof as I was sure that that would bring it on. (By this time I could hardly walk as my feet were sore and I was bruised from my exertions.) So there I was about to leap when I saw Daddy standing by the barn watching me. He asked what on earth was wrong and why was I trying to hurt myself. I started to cry and he took me inside, sat on the rocker and pulled me on his knee. Grannie came in and so did Jamie and Robbie. Dad asked again what was wrong. Finally Jamie walked over and said, "Daddy, Maria's going to have a baby and she was trying to get rid of it." Grannie sat down and everything was deathly still. Finally Daddy jumped up and dropping me to the floor, said, "Who did it?" Jamie grabbed me, sure that Dad was going to kill me and Robbie jumped in front of Dad and said, "Don't hit her. It's not her fault." Dad tried to get hold of me, saying all the time, "I'll kill him, I'll kill him." I was sure that he meant me. By this time the little ones were all in the room, crying hysterically.

Grannie managed to catch Daddy's arm and calmed him down. She told Dolores and Peggie to take the children outside. Dolores' face was terrified and the look in Dad's eyes was awful. Grannie asked why I thought I was pregnant and who the boy was. I didn't know what she was talking about, so she explained, "Maria, you can't be pregnant unless you sleep with a man." When I told her what Robbie had told me she started to laugh and pulled me close, saying, "No, my girl, you are not going to have a baby." Daddy, however, was not so sure, so I was taken to the doctor in town. After he had examined me and talked to me about babies, he spoke with Dad privately for a long time.

On our way home Dad and I talked about babies, men, women and love. I asked him what kind of women men liked—I have to laugh now at his description. It made me feel that I might as well give up right then as there was no way I could ever be the combination of saint, angel, devil and lady that was required. I decided that it was a good thing I liked horses and had a big family to raise as my future with men didn't look very bright.

Soon afterwards we went to visit Cheechum and spent a week with her. I was so happy, for I had so many things to talk over with her, but it seemed we were never alone. Then, the day before we left, she took me with her to dry some meat. While we sat by the fire, I told her about Harold, about how I had thought I was pregnant, and that I was probably going to be an old maid. She gave me some advice: "Your Father, like all men, is a dreamer and that's the key. Don't try to impress them, let them impress you. Be yourself and do what you want. Someday you'll find the one man you belong to—when it happens you'll know." I was quite prepared to take her advice as I had already decided to ignore boys.

Cheechum and I spent the whole day talking. I told her how desperately I wanted to finish school and take everyone away; how I longed for something different for us; how I didn't want to be like our women who had nothing but kids, black eyes and never enough of anything; that I didn't want my brothers to be like the men around us, who just lived each day with nothing to look forward to except the weekend drunks. She didn't say very much, only smiled and said, "Now I know that you belong to me. Don't let anyone tell you that anything is impossible, because if you believe honestly in your heart that there's something better for you, then it will all come true. Go out there and find what you want and take it, but always remember who you are and why you want it."

Chapter 12

Dad had a very beautiful, spirited horse he used for hunting. He was a yearling stallion when Daddy bought him and had never known another rider. When I tried to ride him I got so bruised and battered from being thrown off and chased out of the pasture that Dad decided that I would have to continue to use Ellen's Welsh pony. So I kept it in our pasture, but I had my heart set on King, and any other horse seemed like a nag in comparison. I spent hours watching him, scheming how to win him. Finally, one day I discovered something. Robbie was eating raw turnips and when he happened to drop one, King gobbled it up and looked for more. I raced to the house, peeled a turnip and cut it up into pieces. I went over to the trough and dropped a few on the ground. I did this for several days, always making sure that King knew that I was the one who had dropped them. I would sit on the fence and eat huge pieces of turnip while he watched. Sometimes I would offer him a bite, and soon he was following me around, looking for a handout. In a week, he would even let me saddle him without biting. Then one day I climbed on. He stood still for a few seconds—then I was face down in the dirt. So for two days he had no turnips. He would follow me all over the pasture but I ignored him. The third day I saddled him again, feeding him turnips first. I got on and this time he tossed his head and crowhopped all over the field. I fed him when we got back to the barn and from that day on, I had no problems. He was very spirited and would sometimes take the bit and try to run away, but never to the point where he could not be handled. My brothers tried to ride him, and my uncles and Daddy's friends, but none was successful, and I never volunteered my secret.

Grannie left us just before Christmas and never came back. She was ill with cancer. I had so much to do that I seldom had time to be sorry for myself. The children were getting older and harder to manage. My sisters needed me as they were getting to the age when they wanted pretty dresses and were teased a lot about their poor clothes. No one wanted to housekeep for us as there was just too much to do, not enough to eat, and we could only pay poor wages. We struggled along as best we could and managed to survive that winter.

Sophie, a Halfbreed woman married to a white farmer, lived about a mile from our house. She and her husband were childless, and although Sophie was hardly the motherly type, she was kind and loved children. They were extremely poor as her husband was very lazy. They were also dirty and I doubt whether the house had ever seen soap and water. Their five dogs lived in the shack with them, as well as numerous cats, and in summer the chickens wandered in and out. She was an ugly woman with a huge hooked nose, greyish yellow hair and had scarcely any teeth. She always wore three or four dresses, one on top of the other, rubber boots and a hat. In the summer she wore a white night cap with raggedy lace, and in winter a hood trimmed with fox fur. She always wore bright red lipstick and smeared it on her cheeks as well. She loved to cook, but couldn't, and was the greatest talker. She would even talk for hours to Geordie, our baby. Her husband was skinny and had bumps all over his hands and face. They had lived in the community for years and were considered crazy.

They often came to visit us and insisted that we go to their place for Sunday dinner. I didn't mind Sophie and her husband Andy, but my older brothers and two sisters disliked them. The little boys thought they were great, for when Sophie saw them in the store she'd hug and kiss them and buy them candy.

One Sunday, she invited us for dinner to have roast pork, apple pie and the works. Daddy lined us all up before we left and said that no matter how awful the food, we had to eat it and thank her for it. When we arrived she was bustling around baking pies, with chickens, dogs and cats running around everywhere. It was unbelievable. Andy was so lazy that he didn't even cut firewood. Instead he kept a long piece of wood sticking out of the stove and as it burned up, he pushed it in.

When it was time to eat, all the dogs and cats gathered around the table and watched us. The meat wasn't cooked enough, the potatoes were scorched and the pie crust was soggy and heavy. We managed to get half-way through dinner without too much trouble. We slid our food to the floor for the dogs to eat. As our plates emptied, Sophie gave us more and more, thinking we were too shy to ask for seconds. Just as we were almost finished, Robbie slipped his pie to the floor and the dogs got into a fight. When the commotion was over, Sophie sat down and said, "It sure makes me feel good to have everyone like my cooking so much." We all burst out laughing and she did too, without knowing the reason why.

We had a Christmas concert at school that year, followed by a dance. It was a big social event and Daddy promised to buy me new clothes as this dance would be my first grown-up affair. On the way into Canwood he said that I could pick out my own dress and shoes. At last I could have the red dress I had dreamed about for years. I saw it as soon as we walked into the store—red net over taffeta, sprinkled with silver stars. It had a low v-neckline, a stand-up

collar, short sleeves with winged cuffs, and a tight
waist with at least twenty silver buttons up the front.
Daddy tried to steer me to a more practical rack, but I
tried it on and although it was a little big in the bust,
it fitted otherwise. He bought it for fifteen dollars. I
found the shoes I wanted immediately. They were
high-heeled wedge pumps with thin red, green and
yellow straps across the foot and ankle. I also bought
silk stockings. I had never seen nylons, but my aunts
back home wore silk stockings when they dressed up.

The night of the dance I asked Sophie to come
over and watch the children while I got ready. I
curled my already curly hair with rags and painted
my nails red. After my bath, I undid my rag curlers
and I had fat little curls all over my head. I didn't
comb my hair because I felt that it had an Elizabeth
Taylor effect the way it was. I held up my silk stockings with red rubber jar rings. Sophie gave me her
lipstick and I was ready. She was as excited as I was
and raved about how beautiful I looked. In the mirror
I saw that the bust of my dress was drooping, so I
found some cotton batting and filled my bra so it fit
perfectly.

The family was in the living room, waiting for me
to come down. Daddy was sitting in his rocking chair
and the kids were on the floor. When I came down
everyone just sort of let their breath go. Dad's eyes
filled with tears as I came tottering over in my high-
heeled shoes. He got up and hugged me and said, "If
only Momma could see you now." Dolores said,
"You're beautiful." Jamie and Robbie for once didn't
say a word.

I went to the concert and dance full of confi-
dence. Daddy had insisted that Sophie chaperone
me—that was my only problem. She had on her green
hood and old black coat and I was ashamed of her.
But she was so proud of me that she told everyone
how beautiful I was, almost as if she had invented me.
During intermission, I was standing near the door

with Karen when a girl from school came over and asked loudly, "Is that woman your mother?" Everyone started to snicker and I looked at her and said, "That old, ugly Indian?" and laughed until I saw Sophie's face. She looked so rejected as she walked to a bench and sat down that I felt shame and hatred for her, myself and the people around me. I could almost see Cheechum standing beside me with a switch saying, "They make you hate what you are." My evening was ruined and I left shortly after. Sophie walked home with me and as we got to the door she took my hand and said, "It's okay Maria, I was young once too and I felt like you did." I wanted to throw my arms around her and tell her I loved her, but instead I slapped her hand away and said, "I don't need you. It's all your fault, all of you," and ran inside. I tore my dress taking it off and stuffed it into a trunk along with my shoes. I lay in bed with a lump in my throat, wanting to cry so badly, but not being able to.

Sophie never mentioned that night. When I saw her again I tried to apologize and she said to forget about it. I saw her again, years later, and told her how badly I still felt. She said once again that she understood that I had a right to feel as I did. She told me that she was very sick and knew she was going to die soon, and had thought a lot about me and what had happened that night. She felt bad because she'd never in her life tried to do anything to make her situation better. She said she regretted that instead of trying to improve things for herself and for our people, she had let herself believe she was merely a "no good Halfbreed."

Chapter 13

We were happy to see summer come. Nothing ever seemed so bad when it was warm. Jamie got a full-time job as soon as school was out and Dad was back working Mr. Grey's farm with Bob.

Spring was very hard for us as our vegetables were all gone as were the berries and meat, and we lived mostly on small game such as ducks, rabbits and gophers. Ellen used to pack lunches for Dad to eat in the field and could never understand why he ate so much when he seemed like such a light eater in the house. Dad noticed that a lot of good leftovers got thrown to the pigs so finally he insisted that there was no need for her to make his lunch so early in the morning, that he would make it himself. He took the leftovers and as much as he could of everything else without being obvious. These he would drop off at home on his way from barn chores to the fields, and we would eat them during the day.

We had no housekeeper after April. Jamie and I took turns missing school to baby-sit the younger ones, and because we were in the same grade we were able to help each other with homework at night. After a week, the teacher said if we missed any more days she would have to report us and the family allowance would be cut off. We received fifty dollars a month and used it to buy flour, lard, macaroni, tomato soup, baking powder and tea, and a few other groceries. If we lost that there would be nothing.

We decided to take the little ones with us to school. There was dense bush right behind the school-house and there we left Geordie, Danny and Edward. We used long pieces of baling twine and tied them to trees, told them to be quiet or teacher would see them and put us in the orphanage. Then the five of us at the school ran back and forth every few minutes to the toilets, to check on them. This worked for nearly a month until the teacher began to scold us for using the bathroom so often, and soon the kids were teasing us too. Then came a day when she forbade us to go out during classes. I knew that the little ones would become frightened, so about ten o'clock I asked to go out and was told to wait for recess. I sat there for what seemed like an eternity, and then just ran out. Edward was at the edge of the playground, crying, but afraid to come any closer. I raced past him and found Geordie with the twine twisted around his neck. He was all blue; Danny was crying and trying to loosen the rope. I managed to get him untangled and pounded him on the back. I was sure he was dead but at last he came to, and while hugging him and trying to calm the others saw our teacher standing there. She looked so funny when she asked me what was wrong. I told her then about having no housekeep-er; about our fear of losing the family allowance and maybe ending up in an orphanage. For once, in spite of my dislike for her, I poured everything out.

That evening Ellen and Bob came over and asked us why we had never told them; they said they would have helped us and that that was what friends were for. They did not want to see me leave school and decided to ask Dad if they could adopt the little ones and raise them. We would be nearby and could have seen them all the time. When Dad refused they tried to reason with us, saying that it would be easier and would give us all a better chance. I remember how afraid I became. Those little ones were mine and a part of me. I could not give them away. We were very

close, all of us, and protected and loved each other. So
Ellen and Bob offered help instead—food, clothing;
and said that anything they had we could share. They
also said that some of the neighbours were finding
clothing and vegetables for us. There was a tight knot
in my stomach and a feeling of shame and hate. No
one had ever had anything to do with us, never visited
or invited us over. They had laughed at our clothes
and the way we acted—like "wild colts"—and now
they wanted to give us things. Dad told Bob that he
liked both him and Ellen for their kind treatment. He
said that we would be glad to have them help us and
that some day we would repay them. But he refused
to accept charity from anyone else. He said, "We are
poor but there is no way they are going to make my
children poorer. Maria will just have to quit school till
fall, and we'll manage." I missed my school work and
tried for a long time to do it at home, but eventually
gave up. I just didn't have time and the books only
seemed to taunt me and fill me with a despair I
couldn't handle.

When school was let out I started to work part-
time, cleaning for people for a couple of dollars a day.
Dolores was ten by now and with Robbie's help was
able to manage fairly well around the house. Jamie
gave me his money to help out, and with what Dad
made we ate better than usual. The few dollars I
earned I spent on my two sisters. They had always
worn the awful-looking dresses I made and old black
farm shoes, identical to boys' ones. With my money I
was able to buy them girls' shoes and other little
things to make them feel better. I never felt badly
about the boys, but many times it hurt when I saw
Dolores and Peggie looking at other little girls with
wishful eyes. They were so cute, the two of them, and
very shy. Peggy was tiny with red hair and big blue
eyes. She cried if someone even raised a voice to her,
but was also a real chatterbox when we were alone.
Dolores had brown hair and hazel eyes. She seldom

cried and spent a great deal of time alone. She was more sensitive than Peggie, but never showed her emotions; instead she would run outside and walk around by herself until she was all right.

Robbie was growing up as well and was becoming hard to handle. He was so full of life and adventure. He could find fun and trouble anywhere and always managed to cause either the most hysterical situations for us or get us into trouble. There was seldom a happy medium for him. He was our hunter and would be gone for days on end, coming home only at suppertime, and he was our artist—with his crayons he would make pictures of all the things our people did in every-day life: Daddy skinning beaver; Grannie Dubuque drying meat; sketches of us working around the house. He saved every penny he could get and spent it on pencil crayons. When he was home in the evenings he was always sketching and drawing.

Jamie was quiet, thoughtful and very gentle, unlike the rest of us. He was also very protective. When we had problems he always found a reasonable solution, and without him, many times I wouldn't have been able to carry on.

The three babies were inseparable, and if I held one I had to hold all three. They reminded me of affectionate little puppies, always rolling around and wrestling. Edward was the oldest of the three and looked almost identical to Geordie; they both had brown curly hair and hazel eyes. Danny—well, Danny was different. He had black hair as straight as an Indian's and regardless of how short it was or how well combed, it always stood up like a porcupine. He was as dark as me, with huge eyes. He was always smiling in his sleep and was bigger and sturdier than the others, and much more aggressive. How we all loved those little boys!

My cleaning jobs were back-breaking. I worked on Monday and Tuesday for Mr. Grey's oldest daughter who hated housework and should have been a man. She looked, acted and dressed like one. She was out with the cattle and sheep from early morning till late at night, leaving her three little boys to look after themselves. Her house was always messy and had dirty clothes and dishes piled all over. I had to clean the house, do the washing and ironing, bake twelve loaves of bread and have it all done by Tuesday night. She paid me five dollars, sometimes eight.

She didn't like Indians and talked in front of me as if I were deaf. She would tell her visitors that we were only good for two things—working and fucking, if someone could get us to do it. She made jokes about hot bucks and hot squaws and talked like we were animals in the barnyard. I despised that woman, but because I needed the money I kept my mouth shut and pretended it didn't bother me. Apart from that she wasn't cruel; she used to chat with me and even let me use her horses whenever I wanted. I guess she was just frustrated with her life. Whenever she got a chance she'd go to dances in nearby native communities and sneak off into the bush with the men. I know she made countless passes at Dad. This was common in our area: the white men were crazy about our women and the white women, although they were not as open and forward about it, were the same towards our men.

I worked for different people that summer and I got educated quickly. The other women I worked for weren't as dirty-mouthed as Mr. Grey's daughter, but they were far from friendly. Some watched me in case I stole something; others were afraid I would lead husbands or sons down the garden path. Although I never did, I had all the opportunities in the world. I did work for some people who were kind and paid me well. I was never brought into the family circle, but I was treated fairly and I was satisfied with that. One older Swedish couple was good to me and we got along really well. Eric was a big jovial man who always had lumps of sugar in his pockets for my little brothers, and his wife was nearly as big, with the same happy personality. They told me about Sweden and we talked about the different ways people lived. They were as interested in our people's old way of life as I was in theirs.

Summer was soon over and everyone was preparing for school. We had not found a housekeeper, and so I had given up even dreaming about going back. Two days before school was to start, while Daddy and I were patching pants for the boys, he asked if I really minded not going back. I guess he knew how disappointed I was. Anyway, he left without saying any more and only returned the next night. He had an Indian woman with him. She was a widow in her late thirties with no children. Dad introduced her, then took me outside for a walk while the little ones talked to her. He told me that he was going to live with Sarah, that he had known her for years and that she was a kind, clean, good woman. He wanted me to continue school and said that it would be easier for all of us to have her. He said I would like her and if I couldn't, to try for the sake of the little ones. I was so mixed up and confused. I wanted to go to school so badly, yet I didn't want Daddy to marry anyone. I was afraid she might be mean or else completely take over and that I'd never be able to take the little ones away to the city. When I went inside, Geordie was cuddled up on her knee and the others were all over her, demanding attention. I said nothing and went straight to bed.

When I got up in the morning to prepare breakfast it was all ready and Sarah was bustling around the kitchen as if she had always been there. Dad was right. She was a good cook and very clean, and was good to the kids. She was quiet, and although she talked often to the younger ones, we seldom said more than ten words to each other. I would come home from school and my work would all be done, even my

109

clothes ironed, mended and folded neatly on my bed. There was more time to do the kinds of things I enjoyed, like reading or riding.

Bob and Ellen bought an old truck, so on Saturday nights Jamie, Karen, Robbie and I would go to town with them. I looked forward to the trip all week. St. Michele was a French town with a population of about one thousand which doubled on Saturdays as it was surrounded by two Indian reserves and at least ten Halfbreed settlements. Business depended on Native people. It would be jumping as people came from all over to shop, drink beer, dance and fight. There was a movie house where all the kids and the mothers who didn't drink went and one hotel beer parlour for the men. Women were not allowed in bars then, so those who drank did it in private homes or in back of the livery stable. There was one big general store that sold everything from soup to hammers and harnesses, two small stores, and two coffee shops, one of which stayed open all night on the weekend, a livery stable, a blacksmith shop, a pool hall, a farm implement shop, a car lot, and three Roman Catholic churches and schools. The buildings were all strung out on an unpaved road, with board sidewalks. The French people lived on the south side, the Halfbreeds and Indians in the north and west ends. The two groups didn't live side by side as they never got along, so the two sections were known as Indian and Halfbreed towns.

Early Saturday afternoons were usually quiet and the only people around were the local French and whites from surrounding areas doing their shopping. There was an unwritten law: our people never came in until after four and the whites would then turn the town over to us. They never mixed with us although their revenue depended on Native people's money. Some of the white men stayed, usually the town drunks, the wilder sons and husbands, and a few women. The Frenchmen would never miss a good fight or a Native woman, so they were there too.

110

There was always a feeling of excitement in the air as people started to arrive. They came in wagons as well as broken down cars or trucks, loaded till the springs were dragging, with men, women and children all laughing, talking and singing. The Halfbreeds were noisy, boisterous and gay, while the Indians were quiet and kept to themselves. This of course only lasted until the third bottle of beer. The women did their shopping and visited, while the men all traipsed to the bar. Kids and under-age boys and girls hung around on the street corners, in the pool hall and coffee shops. The stores all closed at six, the show started at eight, the dance at nine. In my younger years the shows were the biggest thrill of my life.

One show I remember was about the Northwest Rebellion. People came from miles around and the theatre was packed. They were sitting in the aisles and on the floor. Riel and Dumont were our heroes. The movie was a comedy and it was awful: the Halfbreeds were made to look like such fools that it left you wondering how they ever organized a rebellion. Gabriel Dumont looked filthy and gross. In one scene his suspenders broke and his pants fell down, and he went galloping away on a scabby horse in his long red underwear. Louis Riel was portrayed as a real lunatic who believed he was god, and his followers were real "three stooges" types. Of course the NWMP and General Middleton did all the heroic things. Everyone around us was laughing hysterically, including Halfbreeds, but Cheechum walked out in disgust. Many years later I saw the movie again and it made me realize that it's no wonder my people are so fucked up.

From the time I was twelve I longed for the night I would be allowed to go to the dance in town. Daddy let me go to the dances at our school with a chaperone. But the dances in town were forbidden. Dad said that I would have to be sixteen and that even then I had better make damn sure he didn't find out about it. He said that it was no place for a decent girl and

111

that only whores went there. I didn't know what a whore was, but whatever it was, it certainly sounded exciting, and I felt that if it was not too wicked for him, then it was good enough for me.

The movie was over at the same time the bar closed. By this time the men would be hammered out of their minds and fights would break out. Gradually everyone would drift to the dance hall, where strains of the "Red River Jig" could be heard. We kids would have to go sleep in the wagons after we got tired of running around, or else go to someone's house and wait. Those little houses would be full at night, with mothers and children sleeping all over the floors, and beds piled high with babies. The parents would start gathering their kids in the early hours of Sunday morning and by ten-thirty the town would be deserted, except for French people heading for Mass.

Karen and I would hope and pray when we went to town that Dad would stay home so we would be free. If he came, we had to toe the line. Regardless of how drunk he might get, he always checked up on us three or four times in an evening. I had met a guy that summer at the horse races and my only chance to see him was each Saturday night when we went to town, and if Dad had known he would probably have grounded me. I was only fifteen and Smoky had a reputation that made even Halfbreeds shake their heads. He was twenty-four and I don't know why he ever noticed me. He was six feet tall, which was tall for a Halfbreed in our part of the country, and he danced, fought and sang through life, laughing even when he was angry or fighting.

I had met him at a horse-jumping competition and races that were being held at a nearby community. Karen and I had both entered and had practised for weeks. I was using our new horse, Brandy, and was sure I could win because he could jump any fence or barricade we put in front of him. I spent hours oiling and polishing my saddle and bridle, and when

Sunday arrived Karen and I left at dawn because we wanted to get there early and rest our horses.

Brandy and I made all the barricades on the first round, and on the second we were leading with only one jump left when I felt the saddle slip. I tried to stop the horse but he was so crazy with excitement that I had no control over him. Just as he jumped the last barricade, the saddle and I flew through the air. I was knocked unconscious and woke up to see the ugliest, most handsome man (Smoky) I had ever seen in my life bending over me. When I tried to get up he laughed and said, "You won the jumping competition. Your horse finished alone when you decided to have a little sleep." I was so excited that I forgot my bruises, my aching head, and that dreamy guy, for I had won fifty dollars. I hobbled over to Brandy and almost cried for joy. Smoky came over with my saddle and showed me the broken cinch which he said he would mend so that I could get home. He asked if I was Danny's sister, and when I replied, "His daughter," he laughed and said, "I guess I'll come and visit your Dad—he's always telling me to drop in."

On the way home Karen was breathless with excitement. She said Smoky was from Batoche and had just come out of the penitentiary that past winter. He had a wild reputation, and though half the women were after him, he had no steady girlfriend. She went on and on, but I was too excited about my fifty dollars to pay any attention. I had not told Dad what I was doing that day, thinking I would surprise him with the money I knew I would win.

I didn't give Smoky much thought for the next few weeks. When I mentioned him to Daddy he hadn't seemed upset, because he probably thought of me still as a little girl. I was home helping Sarah make lye soap one day when Smoky arrived on horseback. He smiled at me and then took his horse to the barn, and spent the rest of the afternoon playing softball with the kids. I was beside myself with excitement and managed to ruin a whole batch of soap. Finally Sarah said she would finish and told me to get supper started. She patted my arm and I blushed all over when I looked at her and realized she knew how I was feeling. Once inside, I raced upstairs to comb my hair and as I was changing my clothes I remembered what Cheechum had told me: "Never ever try to impress a man, be yourself."

I got back into my shirt and jeans and on the way to the kitchen I started wondering whether he had just come to see Daddy. I would make a fool of myself if I acted as if I liked him. So I prepared supper and went about my business as usual. Daddy was happy to see Smoky and invited him to spend a few days with us, and perhaps they would go hunting. During supper I acted as normal as ever, even getting into a fight with Robbie. After the dishes were done, I saddled Brandy and rode over to help Ellen with the milking. Just as I was getting ready to come home Robbie rode in with Smoky and said that they were out for a ride and had stopped to escort me home. On the way, Robbie left us and I was alone for the first time with a man.

That started a new page in my life. It was a man, not a boy, who told me I was beautiful and wanted to see me again. I told him Daddy would never allow it because I had to wait until I was sixteen. He said that was good and that I should not be angry with Dad for making such a rule, that more fathers should do it. He promised to come as often as he could without Dad realizing it was to see me.

Smoky would come for a day or so and go hunting with Daddy. We seldom had a chance to talk, let alone neck, but I was happy and didn't really care. If he came such a distance to see me, then there was nothing to worry about. He came to the school dances and I would spend the whole evening with him under Sarah's watchful eye. Once Sarah could not take me because she was sick, and seeing my disappointment,

Daddy asked Smoky to chaperone me and make sure I did not leave the hall or get too friendly with anyone. I was in seventh heaven, for this was my first real date. For someone with such a terrible reputation, Smoky was a real gentleman. He never drank or got into fights at those dances, so I decided Karen had been really misinformed.

When Karen and I went into town, Ellen and Bob did not worry about us as they assumed that our boyfriends were classmates. They did not tell Daddy that I didn't always go to the show. Then one night he found out and there was hell to pay.

I had begged Smoky to take me to the dance for a little while instead of the movie, and finally he gave in. He picked me up at the theatre about eight and Karen and her boyfriend came with us. I smelled whiskey on his breath, but in the excitement didn't give it any thought. The hall was full when we arrived and everything looked normal, much to my disappointment. I had expected something wicked. The music was wonderful, different from the school dances. No one can play a fiddle and guitar like a Halfbreed. They can make these instruments come alive—laugh, cry and shout. I danced every dance. It was almost as if I had been asleep for fifteen years and had suddenly awakened. I knew nearly everyone there and wondered why Daddy had forbidden me to come.

Smoky tried to make me leave about eleven o'clock, but I coaxed him to stay till midnight as I knew Bob and Ellen would not leave without us. About eleven-thirty people started coming in from the bar—white people as well—and you could almost cut the tension with a knife. When a Frenchman came over and grabbed me for a waltz, Smoky told him to leave me alone. Everything happened so fast: it seemed that one minute Smoky was leading me away and the next everyone was shouting and fighting, and he was gone. Karen came over and pulled me back.

Smoky and the Frenchman were fighting, and because Smoky was winning, a whole group of French guys started to kick and beat him. I couldn't stand watching so I grabbed a stove poker and waded right in. I ended up exchanging blows with a white woman and then saw Dad and a couple of men coming to Smoky's rescue. When the fight was over, Daddy saw me and went purple with rage. He looked at Smoky and said, "She's my daughter, what the hell are you doing here with her? I'll settle with you later," and with that he dragged me over to the truck where Ellen and Bob were waiting. They took Karen and me straight home. I was worried sick wondering what Daddy would do with Smoky and what was going to happen to me when he got home.

Dad got home Sunday afternoon and called me to his room. He warned me that if I ever saw Smoky again he would beat me until I couldn't walk. He said Smoky was only trouble and I was too young to get mixed up with a grown man, especially one with such a reputation. He said if he ever came around again he'd break his goddamn back. When I tried to interrupt, I was told to shut up. He said that I had acted like a common whore. "Your mother never did anything like that in her life, and as long as you're under my roof you'll act like a lady." Finally I got angry and shouted that if he could go to such places, then why couldn't I; that if Smoky was good enough to be his best friend why wasn't he good enough for me? I told him I was a Campbell, not a Dubuque and if Mom was a lady then why did she run off with him? I had never talked back before, much less yelled at him. He slapped my face and knocked me over a chair, and when he went to slap me again, I said, "You're not so hot. You're living with that woman when you should be married to her, so don't tell me what's right and wrong." He got a hurt look on his face and walked out.

My relationship with Dad changed after that, and

we had many more fights. We seemed to drift apart and our closeness was gone. I disobeyed his rules whenever I wanted to and fought back when he got angry with me. I made life miserable for Sarah, who did her best to keep peace between us.

I continued to go to the dances in town whenever Karen and I could sneak away from Ellen, not because I really wanted to, but because Daddy had said no. I always looked for Smoky at these dances and finally one night I saw him come in—with a woman. He tried to talk to me, but all I wanted to do was hurt him. He said that Dad had told him to leave me alone until I was seventeen. Then if we wanted to see each other we could, and when I was eighteen he said we could get married. I remember looking at him and saying, "Marry you? You've got to be joking! I'm going to do something with my life besides make more Half-breeds."

I wanted to cry. I couldn't understand what was wrong with me. I loved Smoky and wanted to be with him forever, yet when I thought of him and marriage I saw only shacks, kids, no food, and both of us fighting. I saw myself with my head down and Smoky looking like an old man, laughing only when he was drunk. I loved my people so much and missed them if I couldn't see them often. I felt alive when I went to their parties, and I overflowed with happiness when we would all sit down and share a meal, yet I hated all of it as much as I loved it.

Chapter 14

The relief people were at our house one afternoon when I came home from school. They told Dad he had been reported for living in common-law with Sarah, and along with all the other reports they had received over the years they would have to do something this time. Dad didn't speak for a long time. Finally he said, "If Sarah leaves, will you help me with an allowance of some kind, so I can stay home? I don't want Maria quitting school." The man answered, "No, I'm sorry, Mr. Campbell. We can only help widows. You're healthy and you can work. You'll have to marry this woman or we'll just have to take the kids."

Dad and I sat down for the first time in months and talked without getting mad at each other. I told him that he could either marry Sarah or I could quit school—anything so we would not get sent to an orphanage. He told me not to worry, that we'd work something out.

The next day Sarah said she was leaving us, that Dad really didn't want to marry her and that she and the kids were getting too attached to each other. She said she'd stay until school was finished in June so I could finish grade eight. That was the most I had ever heard her say at one time.

June came and Sarah left us. Daddy seemed to be in a daze after that, and although he worked, he was very depressed. I asked him why he wouldn't marry Sarah. He said that he couldn't, that Mom was the only woman he had ever loved. Nothing more was ever said, and again the responsibility for the family was left to me.

Jamie and I had long talks those first few weeks about what we would do. Bob was going to visit a sister in Blue River, so Jamie decided he would go to British Columbia with him and look for work. He could make nearly four hundred dollars a month out there, and we couldn't live on what he and Dad made at home.

Dad said nothing when Jamie told him he was leaving and I doubt if he even heard him. Jamie was fourteen years old. He got a job as section man on the railroad and, true to his word, he sent money home each month. He didn't make four hundred but it was still a fortune to us. I got a job as a clerk in a store and Dolores looked after the house. Then the relief people came again and said they were going to put us in three separate homes.

Daddy just didn't seem to understand what was happening to us and I was sick with fear. The relief man said I was too young to look after all of us, so I wrote Jamie that night and asked him to come home. He arrived a week later and we tried to make plans. We talked of moving to B.C., but we had no money to go anywhere. There was only one alternative. I would have to get married. Then they wouldn't be able to say I was too young to care for a family. I thought of Smoky, but knew he had nothing, and we had to find someone who wanted to take over a large family and could afford to support all of us.

I found my man a couple of weeks later. He came into the store one evening and spent nearly an hour talking to me. I could tell by his expensive clothes and new car that he could afford to keep us all. He was originally from Saskatchewan but lived in Vancouver. He had just come back to sell the farm left to him by his parents.

Darrel and I became engaged on the first of October. Daddy tried to talk me out of it, saying that if I was going to marry, to marry Smoky because he loved me and was one of my own people. He said that I might never have much, but at least I would be happy. When I refused to change my mind, Dad answered, "I won't give you my permission to get married. You're under age." So I told him the only thing I knew which would make him change his mind. I lied and said, "I'm going to have a baby. You have to let me." That was it. I was married on October 27th, 1955. I had a husband and I could keep my brothers and sisters. I was fifteen years old.

Halfbreeds love weddings, so my aunts and uncles made plans for the big day and arranged the marriage at the Catholic church. But I refused to have anything to do with the Church, saying that if it would not take my mother, it would never be good enough for me. The wedding and reception and dance would all have to be held in the school, and instead of the priest, I wanted the Anglican minister who had come to Momma's funeral. My aunts were horrified! No one got married in a school when there was a church! I told them that no one had a funeral outside a churchyard either. My mind was made up, and as they loved me they set about to get the school decorated and to do the baking and cooking.

Everyone was upset, but I didn't care. I felt that our people forgot the slaps they got from the Church too easily. I was only concerned with getting married as fast as I could, before Darrel changed his mind about the prospects of inheriting six children.

My wedding day came, and by then I realized that I didn't even like the man who was to be my husband. Karen was my bridesmaid and knew how I felt. She tried to stop me, and said she'd even quit school if it would help us. She threatened to tell Dad that I wasn't pregnant, but I knew that if I wanted anything better for myself and family other than an orphanage, foster home, or mud shack, I had to go through with it.

The whole day was a nightmare for me. Darrel's sisters came and were upset when they saw I wasn't white, and were horrified with the "drunken Breeds" at the reception. Cheechum was heart-broken; she refused to come when she heard that Darrel was white, saying that nothing good ever comes from a mixed marriage. She had hoped that Smoky and I would marry, and if she had still been living with us we probably would have. Smoky was a great friend of Cheechum's and he loved her very much.

Dad broke down and cried before the wedding started. My aunts all cried. The only ones who were happy were my brothers and sisters who sat in the front row, smiling and excited. Even though I wanted to run away, I couldn't do it, because I knew they completely depended on me. The schoolhouse was crowded to overflowing. Dad's friends and relatives had come from as far away as Isle La Crosse to see his first-born marry. There was more food than I had seen in a long time and enough liquor to last a month—homemade whiskey, wine, and kegs of beer that Darrel had supplied.

Smoky came in just after midnight and everyone became quiet. My uncle went over to him but he pushed him aside saying, "I didn't come here to fight. I came to say good-bye to Maria." He turned to me and said, "What the hell are you doing here? You're supposed to be gone. You don't want to leave us, do you?" Then he turned to Darrel and shook his hand. He told me as he was leaving that if things didn't work out to come home. I wanted to leave with him but couldn't, and suddenly the realization of what I had done hit me and I felt like crying.

I didn't want to leave so we stayed until five o'clock in the morning, and I'm sure I must have been the only bride from our settlement who cried as she left her wedding dance. We stayed at Darrel's aunt's house in Roseville and the next day drove to Saskatoon for our honeymoon. It was the farthest place I had ever been in my life.

We came back a week later to look for a house in Prince Albert, but ended up in Kettle River. That was my first surprise. Darrel said he'd be out of money soon because his sisters were upset over our marriage, and he had to take an available job there. We rented the top floor of a big two-storey house and brought my brothers and sisters home to live with us. Jamie went back to B.C. to work and promised to send money regularly.

Everything was all right for the first couple of months, but then Darrel began to drink. Soon he lost his job and had to find another. I was pushed around the first few times he was drunk, but then he started to beat me whenever the mood hit him. The children were frightened and Robbie would try to protect me. I became pregnant in the spring and was so sick I could hardly move. Dad knew by then that I had lied about being pregnant before, but he didn't know about the beatings.

One night he was staying with us when Darrel came home drunk and in an ugly mood. He slapped me and I fell down the stairs. I was taken to the hospital because the doctor was afraid I would lose the baby. However, I was okay except for a sprained ankle and a broken wrist. When I got home Daddy had beaten Darrel up, and he didn't hit me again for a long time. The rest of the year was grim. Darrel would be gone for days at a time and when he came home he would jeer at me and call me a fat squaw. The children were unhappy and confused, and did badly in school.

One night in December Darrel came home beaten and covered with blood. Smoky had laid a licking on him. After slapping me, he threw me on the floor and kicked me. He told me to pack up my clothes and kids and move in with that fucking Half-breed—that the kid was probably Smoky's anyway. I ended up in the hospital and Daddy was with me the next morning when Lisa was born. It was a miracle she even lived.

I had no choice but to go home with the baby to Darrel. I didn't know what else to do with the kids, and I was afraid they'd be taken away if I tried to raise them by myself. But I made up my mind that things would be different, that I wasn't going to let Darrel walk all over me any more. I opened up a charge account with Eaton's catalogue and chose expensive Christmas gifts for everyone and new clothes for myself and the kids.

Darrel still drank, but he didn't beat me any more and things started to settle down. Everyone seemed quite happy but somehow I knew that something bad was going to happen.

Darrel was in Prince Albert the day the welfare people came. We were all home and the children were eating lunch when a station wagon pulled up. I looked out the window and I knew that this was it. It was all over. The kids started to cry and hang on to me, but they were pulled away and were in the wagon within a few minutes. I couldn't move. I felt like a block of stone. The wagon drove away with six little faces pressed to the windows, crying for me to help them. I walked around in a daze. Everything went to pieces inside. Dad found me lying on the bed while my baby screamed with hunger.

Nothing was the same after that. Darrel drank more and more, and one night told me that he was the one who had phoned the welfare. He said he knew I had married him because of the kids. I tried to get the children back, but was told to leave them alone. I couldn't even get their addresses to write them. They had been placed in permanent foster homes by the court, and Dad and I weren't even allowed to know where they were.

Darrel announced one day that we were leaving. He said that he was going to take me to Vancouver, and when I didn't respond he said, "What's the matter with you? You always wanted to go to the big city."

That day a friend looked after Lisa while I drove home to the house I grew up in. Dad had moved back there after we lost the children. I told him that I felt responsible for what had happened to the kids and that I was sorry for all the trouble I'd caused him. I said I was leaving and would never come back. He held me close and said not to blame myself, that it was not my fault because he had failed me more.

I lay in bed that night and listened to the frogs sing. I thought of my Cheechum, whose strength and comfort I so desperately missed. I couldn't go to her because I was ashamed. Everything had gone so wrong.

Chapter 15

We stopped in Kristen, Alberta, early one morning, where Darrel said we would be spending a few days with his sister Bonny and her family, before going on to Vancouver. Bonny was Darrel's older sister whom I had met at our wedding. I knew she didn't like or approve of me and I was frightened to death of her. She was very beautiful, very poised and sophisticated, and also very cold. She met us at the station, and as soon as she walked up to us I felt backward, stupid and clumsy. She could always make me feel this way. She never had to say anything. She was happy to see Darrel and Lisa, making a big fuss over them. However she completely ignored me once she had said hello.

I felt very lonely on our drive to their ranch. The country seemed so barren and unfriendly. There was nothing except miles and miles of grain or grazing cattle, and the wind seemed to blow forever.

Their home was beautiful—just like Bonny. I met her husband and two children, and realized at once that she made them feel as I did. She criticized her husband and daughter constantly. It seemed they never did anything right. Her two-year-old son was spoiled and allowed to get away with anything.

Bonny disliked me and didn't go out of her way to hide the fact from anyone. When she realized I was afraid of electrical appliances she insisted I use them, and made jokes about my fear of them, as well as about all my other shortcomings, to people who visited her. She would tell her daughter to do something, and if Betty made a mistake, would say, "Do you want to end up like Maria?"

She also did a lot of drinking, and drank liquor like we drank tea at home. Whenever she'd been drinking too much she would insinuate to Darrel that I was after her husband, and Darrel of course believed her.

Darrel and Bonny left one morning to go to Calgary, and the house seemed to change as soon as they left. It was almost as though we had been prisoners and were finally allowed outside for some fresh air. Bonny returned a couple of days later. She had been drinking and was in a really bad mood. She was no sooner in the house when she told me I was getting out—right away. She said Darrel wasn't coming back, and that he'd told her she was to have Lisa. She said I'd lost my brothers and sisters because I wasn't fit to look after them, and she would have no trouble proving I wasn't fit for Lisa either. I didn't really understand what she was talking about until she started to throw my clothes outside. When I started to pick Lisa up, she tried to stop me. I lost all control of myself then and struck her. I threatened to kill her if she touched my baby. John finally separated us and got Lisa and me into the car. Bonny was standing outside screaming that I'd ruined her brother's life, that I was nothing but a dirty Indian Breed. I felt like I was in a nightmare, and if I'd just wake up it would all go away.

John drove us to the home of some people he knew, and they agreed to hire me as a housekeeper. He gave me fifty dollars, tried to apologize, and finally left. Mrs. Thompson was a good person and I liked her. My work wasn't hard and I was alone all day. However it wasn't long before Mr. Thompson started dropping in and trying to get friendly. I knew what would happen if I stayed and so one day I took Lisa and left. I found out later that they had never
126

been able to keep a girl for very long. He would bother the girls, who would either accept his advances and get fired, or walk out.

I knew no one in the community and I had only twenty-five dollars left of the money John had given me, so I checked into a hotel. I had never looked for a job in my life, so I didn't have sense enough to look in a paper. I was too shy and scared to go into a store and ask if they needed help, and even if I had, what was I to do with Lisa? I stayed at the hotel till I had no money left, then I asked the hotel man to keep my clothes. I didn't know where I was going or what I was going to do. I walked around for most of the day with Lisa. She was hungry and crying but I had no food for her except a bottle of milk. I was walking past a restaurant when I saw a sign in the window that said "Waitress Wanted." I went inside and sat down. An old Chinese man came over and asked me what I wanted. I told him I was looking for a job and had seen his sign. He said he was sorry but he had just hired someone. Lisa was crying, and listening to the old man say he already had someone made me realize that this was it. I didn't even have enough money for coffee, so I couldn't stay there. The old man looked impatient while he waited for me to order something. I didn't know what to do so I started to cry. A young man came out with an old woman and they tried to talk to me, but once I'd started to cry I couldn't stop. The old man brought me some coffee and gave me a cigarette, and finally I was able to tell them what was wrong. As I talked the young man translated what I said to the woman, who immediately put her arm around me. They took us to the kitchen, and while I had some soup and Chinese food, the woman changed Lisa and fed her. When I was through, Lisa was asleep in a banana crate. The young man said his name was Leonard. He lived here with his Mom and Dad, and Grandpa Sing. He said I could have the job and live with them. They didn't

127

have very much, he said, but they wanted me to know I was welcome. The old woman patted my shoulder and smiled and I started to cry again. I'd thought no one gave a damn, and here they were giving me a home, a job, everything.

The café was open from nine in the morning till midnight, but was not busy except on weekends, when people would come in for Chinese food. Lisa was happy and comfortable in an old highchair in the kitchen, where Mama Sing talked and sang to her all day. I'd never known any Chinese people before. There had been one old man in Kettle River who ran a café. People said he ate cats, had lots of money and was extremely dangerous. They said he'd even killed a man once with a meat cleaver. But these people were kind and happy. Their food was delicious, and their home above the café, although not fancy, was comfortable and cosy. I grew very fond of them, as they did of Lisa and me. They sent money home to relatives in China each month, and I learned they had other children there too. Grandpa Sing told me he was going back to China someday, to die there. He and I became very close. Grouchy as he looked, he was a very fine and gentle man. He taught me to play poker and chess when the café was empty. I often thought of them when I'd gone to bed. They never had company except for Mama Sing's brother who came once a month to visit them.

Most of the people who came to the café were friendly enough in a strange kind of way. Sometimes when they were drunk they called them "chinks" or "yellow bastards," or would say things like, "Hey Sing, this meat tastes like dog. You sure you haven't been killing any strays?" I knew Grandpa Sing gave many people money when they were down and out or just short. He knew he would never be paid back but he continued to do it. Yet those very same people laughed at him and treated him as though he were a nitwit who had no feelings. Many times in my life after I left them, when I was full of hate and bitterness, I'd try to think of Grandpa Sing and make myself remember that there were some good people like him in the world.

A rodeo cowboy called Bob used to come to the restaurant a lot when he was in town. He was one of the few men who treated Grandpa like a man. He would sit and visit with him or play cards. He asked me several times to go to a movie with him, but I always refused. It wasn't that I didn't want to go, because I liked Bob, but I was afraid I'd run into Bonny. Kristen was a small town and I knew she'd done a lot of talking about me already. Most of the people believed her and I was aware of the hostility of the women of the town toward me. I didn't want to see her because I didn't know how to cope with her.

Finally Mama Sing told me I should go with Bob. She said it wasn't good for me to stay home all the time. She'd known Bob since he was a boy and he was a good man. When I told her about Bonny she said Bonny didn't go to movies, so I went. I enjoyed Bob's company. He was fun to be with, and when he asked me to go to a dance with him the following Friday, I said yes. It had been a long time since I'd danced and even the thought of Bonny couldn't have kept me away. We arrived at the dance and it was wonderful to be young again and just dance, but it was over all too soon. Bonny arrived with a crowd of people and it was obvious she had been drinking. She saw me and came over. Bob didn't know anything about our relationship and ended up being caught in the middle of a really bad scene. I never went out with Bob after that. I refused to see or talk to him.

I started drinking and partying a lot. I figured "What's the use?"—people believed I was bad anyway, so I might as well give them real things to talk about. Not too long after that Darrel arrived, saying he was sorry and that he wanted us to come back with him.

This time everything would be different. I said yes. I just wanted to get out of Kristen. I didn't care how.

The Sings were very upset. They told me not to go, that Vancouver was a big, ugly city and that something bad would happen to us. Mama Sing asked me then if I would leave Lisa with her at least until I got settled in a home. But I said no. Lisa was all I had in the world. I knew Darrel would leave me again, and if I left Lisa here, how on earth would I ever get back to get her? Then there was the fear of Bonny. I knew she'd come as soon as she heard I'd left Lisa and these people would never be able to fight her. They were too gentle.

Grandpa Sing gave me a gift before I left. Inside a little black box was a jade necklace, earings and bracelet set in an old-fashioned gold setting. He said, "Someday when Lisa grows up, give it to her, and tell her it belonged for generations to my wife's family in China." He told me to call him if I ever needed help. I never saw Grandpa Sing again. Many years later I saw Leonard and he told me that Grandpa had returned to China and had died there.

Chapter 16

Vancouver! It was raining when we arrived. The city was beyond my wildest imagination! It seemed to go on without end. As we drove along in the cab, I pressed my face against the window and drank in everything around me. There were miles and miles of flashing signs and street lights and the tallest buildings in the world. The people all looked rich and well-fed. The store windows were full of beautiful displays, lots of food, clothes and all the things a person could possibly need to be happy.

I sat back and thought, "Maybe it's possible now to bring the kids here, where everything will be clean and good for them." My childhood dreams of toothbrushes and pretty dresses, oranges and apples, and a happy family sitting around the kitchen table talking about their tomorrow came to an abrupt end as I looked out of the window again and saw that we were now in an older part of the city. The buildings kept getting dirtier and dirtier. I had lived in poverty and seen decay but nothing like what surrounded me now.

The cab pulled up in front of a grimy old apartment block and as Darrel paid the driver I looked about. The street was filthy and I shivered and felt sick as I saw the people who were there. They looked poorer than anyone I'd seen at home; there were drunks, and men who walked aimlessly and seemed not to see anything or anyone; women who appeared as though they had endured so much ugliness that nothing could upset them; and pale, skinny, raggedy kids with big, unfeeling eyes who looked so unloved and neglected. Small as they were, they were frightening.

The apartment was up two flights of garbage-littered stairs, and the whole place smelled of stale food, dirty bodies and mould. Our apartment had a small living room with a broken-down chesterfield that served as our bed, and a few pieces of old dirty furniture. The kitchen was just big enough for a folding table, a hot plate, a sink and an old fridge. The bathroom was down the hall and we shared it with all the other tenants on that floor.

I tried my best to clean the place but it made no difference. The kitchen was full of cockroaches which scattered when the light was switched on. Sometimes I had to wait half an hour to use the bathroom. Just waiting was an experience in itself. The most rejected-looking people would be waiting their turns with me. Some tried to be friendly but mostly they were so lost in a world of their own that I doubt if they even saw me. I wondered, as I waited, whether any of them had parents who loved them, or if they had ever laughed, or loved, or hated.

If Darrel had a job he never told me. He would sleep nearly all day and then leave and not return until the early morning. He never talked to me, only answered yes or no to my questions. I tried to stay busy, but there was really nothing to do and no one to talk to except Lisa. By now she was pale and quite miserable, for she was used to being outdoors in the fresh air and sunshine. I had taken her out once when we first arrived, but after being stopped on the street by a man who desperately wanted money, I was too frightened to go out again.

Darrel came home one day and said we were going to a party that evening. He'd even arranged for a baby-sitter to come in to look after Lisa.

We walked into a noisy, smokey apartment full of people drinking and talking. Darrel left me at the door without introducing me to anyone so I sat by myself in the corner. A tall, auburn-haired, striking-looking woman came over and started to talk to me. I liked Lil immediately and we talked about all sorts of things—books, clothes and Lisa. I told her how miserable and disappointed I felt about our life in Vancouver. Before we left she gave me her phone number and we agreed to get together some day soon.

Things between Darrel and me got much worse till finally one day he just didn't come home. After about a week, I knew he wasn't ever coming back and I was in a panic. I was back to no money, no groceries, the rent was due and I had no one to turn to. Then I remembered Lil.

I could say at this point that I was innocent and had no idea what I was getting into. I have even tried to make myself believe this but that would be lying. I did know. I guess I knew from the moment I picked up the phone and called her. There was all the opportunity in the world to run away those first few months, but instead I made myself believe that one day I would wake up and there would be all the things in life which were important to me.

I feel an overwhelming compassion and understanding for another human being caught in a situation where the way out is so obvious to others but not to him. Dreams are so important in one's life, yet when followed blindly they can lead to the disintegration of one's soul.

Take for example the driving ambition and dream of a little girl telling her Cheechum, "Someday my brothers and sisters will each have a toothbrush and they'll brush their teeth every day and we'll have a bowl of fruit on the table all the time and, Cheechum, they'll be able to do anything they want and go anywhere, and every day we'll have a glass of milk and cookies and talk about what they want to do. There will be no more mud shacks and they'll walk with their heads high and not be afraid." The little girl's

133

Cheechum would look at her and see the tooth-brushes, fruit and all those other symbols of white ideals of success and say sadly, "You'll have them, my girl, you'll have them."

The first few days seemed like a dream. Lil made arrangements for Lisa to stay at a convent where the nuns would take good care of her. They were gentle and kind and I knew she'd be safe with them.

I moved into Lil's house in North Vancouver and she took me to a fashionable dress shop where I was fitted with clothes I never thought I'd wear, and to a beauty parlour where my hair was cut and styled. When I was finally pushed in front of a mirror, I hardly recognized the woman staring back at me. She looked cold and unreal, rich and expensive. "Dear God," I thought, "this is how I've always wanted to look, but do the women who look like this ever feel like I do inside?" I wanted to run away, and yet I had to stay.

I lost something that afternoon. Something inside of me died. Life had played such a joke. I had married to escape from what I'd thought was an ugly world, only to fine a worse one. Someday, for certain, I would leave. How, I didn't know, but until then I would do what I had to do.

Lil arranged it so my clientele consisted of older, mature men who thought nothing of spending a small fortune. She was an unusual woman. She was kind in her own way, and I got along well with her. Although the girls at the house ate, talked and lived together, no one ever got very close. Each one of us lived in our own little world.

One Chinese girl, who was part Indian, tiny, fragile and very pretty, had started work a few weeks before I did and was so quiet and gentle that I often wondered how she could stay and not go to pieces. Her room was next to mine and she cried a lot by herself. When I heard her I'd desperately want to go to her and help, but it was impossible. I knew, during all that time in Vancouver, that if I shed even one tear, I would fall apart and be finished. I felt that I'd never be able to pull myself together again so I would try to shut out the sounds of her weeping.

One afternoon she was missing at the table for dinner so I went to her room and knocked. When there was no answer, I opened the door. She was on the floor—dead. She looked so little, so defenseless and young. I stood there, filled with so much hate I was almost sick. She had died from an overdose of drugs. They gave her a welfare burial, and forgot about her.

Chapter 17

Most of the girls at Lil's used pills, and once I discovered them the world became a great deal more bearable. I took them like they were going out of style. They helped me to sleep, they kept me happy, and most of all, I could forget about yesterday and tomorrow. I make it sound as though they were really great, but they only helped for a little while. Once my body grew accustomed to them all they did was make me feel worse. But I continued to take them because by that time I was hooked and couldn't go on without always believing that they would make me feel really good like they had in the beginning. But they never did. I only ended up feeling numb and depressed.

By the time Lil took her share of the money I earned, and I had paid for my clothes, Lisa's room and board, and my pills, which were very expensive, I had no money left and my dreams of saving a lot of money just seemed to get farther and farther away. So when one of the men I'd met through Lil asked me to leave her and let him look after me, I agreed. Mr. ——— was a very wealthy and influential man in Vancouver. He treated me well, gave me a lovely apartment, beautiful clothes, jewellery, and as far as I can remember just about anything else. He brought many of his friends to our apartment and I met important men in both politics and big business. They were all men who saw Lil's girls, and who on many occasions brought them to our place.

When I think back to that time and those people, I realize now that poor people, both white and Native, who are trapped within a certain kind of life, can never look to the business and political leaders of this country for help. Regardless of what they promise, they'll never change things, because they are involved in and perpetuate in private the very things that they condemn in public.

I was using pills and drinking a lot, but instead of finding any escape, I became more and more depressed, and began to hate myself. At times I was utterly lonely—there was no one to talk to. Mr. —— was out of town a lot and even if he were there, he didn't want to listen to my problems. He wanted a good-looking woman to entertain him, and I'd better be damned beautiful and happy and entertaining when he arrived or I'd be out on my ass hustling on the street.

I seldom went out, but one night one of the girls from Lil's called me. She was going to a party at a boost can and asked me to come with her. A boost can is a place where you can meet other people like yourself and visit, relax, do dope, play cards, dance, anything. I'd been doing a little dope by this time, but I wasn't on to any heavy drugs, just grass and sniffing cocaine once in a while. However that night I did heroin, and I forgot everything. It put me into a beautiful world full of beautiful people with no feelings of guilt or shame. I wanted to stay that way, so from that night on I continued to use it, and soon I was hooked.

To live in that dream world meant I had to have enough money to pay for it. Heroin meant money and lots of it. That kind of money meant I had to keep the man who was keeping me happy. To keep him happy meant I had to keep my beauty and sex appeal. Heroin, unfortunately, doesn't improve either one. I soon started to go downhill. I sold my clothes and jewellery just as fast as I got them and became more desperate as each day went by, worrying about tomorrow and my next fix. By this time my sole obsession was dope. I didn't care anymore about anything, not even my baby. I didn't hate, love, or care. Nothing mattered. I was like a block of ice—I had no feelings.

Then I met Ray. I was introduced to him at a boost can party one night. He'd done a lot of time when he was young but somehow had gotten smart as he got older. He was now owner of a construction company and owned real estate and a lot of other things. He knew all the right people and belonged to all the right clubs. I saw him often and he'd take me on drives or to dinner. He knew I was using dope but never said anything. He even helped me out a few times when I had no money.

Then after I'd known him about a month he took me on a drive through all of Vancouver's dead ends. We spent the afternoon and evening in boost cans, dirty cafés, back alleys, cat houses and crash pads. We visited derelicts and dope addicts living in conditions that were unbelievable. When we finally got back to his apartment he asked me if I'd ever thought of kicking. He said he'd help me get straightened out, get a place of my own where I could have Lisa with me. He'd help me go home if I wanted to go home. If I didn't want to help myself, well, he'd tried, but he wouldn't see me anymore either.

I agreed because I was high and I didn't know what I was in for. I knew it would be rough, but never in my wildest dreams did I realize just how rough it would actually be.

Ray took me back to my apartment and I packed all my things. I knew Mr. —— was going to leave me very soon, if he hadn't already gone, so it was better that I got out now. I was sure that, regardless of what happened, I'd be in no worse mess with Ray than I was going to be in very soon anyway.

Ray took me to the home of a woman he knew. She was scarred up and old. She'd been an addict once but had straightened herself out. I didn't know

138

anything about her or her relationship with Ray. She was very gentle and stayed with me through the whole thing.

I could try to describe what happened to me but I really don't know how. Many people have written many things about withdrawal, but writing it can't describe the pain, ugliness and terror you go through. When it was all over and I was well enough to get around, Ray took me to his apartment. He said I'd have to decide what I was going to do. If I wanted to go home he would give me the money or I could work for him, make some fast money and do what I wanted with it.

I had never told Ray about my home or family, and I didn't bother to tell him now why I couldn't go back. What could I go back to? My father was in the bush with no permanent home, and I didn't know where my brothers and sisters were. I'd thought I was too good for my people; I had married so I could have something better. They all knew that when I left them and they would never forget. Yes, they'd take me in and share with me because that was their way, but I would never be one of them again. And my Chee-chum! How could I go home and say to her I'd failed! My home and my people were a part of my life that I wanted to forget, and if calling myself French or Spanish or anything else would help I would do so.

So I stayed and went to work for Ray. I found an apartment, and then came the day I was to pick Lisa up. I hadn't seen her for over four months. I didn't know if she would remember me but my biggest fear was myself. I had reached a point where nothing mattered; I felt no emotion about anything and because I felt this way I knew I could lay off drugs. I really didn't need an escape anymore. I had nothing to escape from. I was afraid I wouldn't feel anything for her either and if I did feel something, what would happen? I'd be full of guilt and shame and I'd end up on dope again. I begged Ray, telling him I wasn't ready for her yet, but he was firm, saying I needed Lisa as much as she needed me.

When we arrived at the convent I wanted to run away, but Lisa was waiting on the steps with one of the sisters. She remembered me, and suddenly it didn't matter anymore. I loved her.

We settled down in our apartment and Ray found me a housekeeper to live in, as my work often took me out of town. He told me I would be making trips to the States to pick up some things. He told me never to ask questions and never talk to the contacts I made. He said the less I knew about him and what I was doing the better. I hardly ever went to a large city, usually to small towns, and I travelled by train, car, bus and plane.

I never carried anything anywhere, except on the underclothes I was wearing—padded bras and girdles. Customs never paid any attention to my underclothes and never searched me. I never discussed my trips with Ray. I just did as he told me and kept my mouth shut.

I knew nothing about him, where he was from or what he did, although I had a good idea. He often got telephone calls at the apartment. One I remember in particular. The phone rang early about four a.m. I woke up and heard him say, "Break his hands, and if that doesn't work, do the same to his arms and legs." I pretended to be asleep, and made up my mind that there was no way I wanted to know more than I did. He travelled often to Montreal and to Ontario, sometimes staying away for a week. I never met any of the men he made deals with, but I attended parties with him and met many government people as well as the businessmen I'd met before.

I told Ray one evening that I had enough money saved and that I wanted to leave. He said that that was our deal, and that if I was ready to go he wouldn't stop me. He told me that he loved me and that maybe it was best that I go. I thought to myself,

"Love! They all love you if they're on the gravy train. He can afford to love me. I made him good money." I neither hated nor loved him. He was a means to an end, and I didn't feel I owed him anything.

Lisa and I left one afternoon on the train for Calgary. I found a small suite and a baby-sitter and started looking for a job. I was in for a surprise—I had no education, no trade, no job experience. Soon my money began to run out and still I had no prospects. I was determined not to go on the street again, and so sought help from the Welfare Department. But they told me that I was considered a resident of B.C. and would have to return there.

I was almost broke, and becoming desperate. The rent was paid for three months, but there would soon be no money for groceries. One afternoon I decided to go to the race track with my baby-sitter's mother and there I won fifty dollars. I met a really nice guy there that day and we went out often after that. Even though I later found out he was a priest, I didn't care—he was good to me.

But I was in a real state of depression by this time, and started taking pills and drinking heavily again—anything to forget about that needle that would let me forget everything. I was so afraid I'd end up back on the street that I started to think about what my Mom had told me about God and churches, so I decided to approach the minister of a nearby United Church. He was a nervous little man who kept fidgeting and blowing his nose. He didn't make me feel very confident, but I went ahead and told him about myself: that I was a drug addict; that I had come from Vancouver; that I had a child and needed help. He kept saying, "My gosh, my gosh!" When my story was finished he said he couldn't help me and he knew of no place I could go for help. However he offered to phone the police as they might know what to do. I told him to forget it and left, more discouraged and depressed than ever. I walked and walked for a long time, and when I got home it was almost morning. That day I called my priest friend and borrowed some money from him. I took the next train back to Vancouver and Lisa went back to the nuns at the convent.

Chapter 18

I had only been in Vancouver a few days when I met a guy just out of the Pen. I went to Mexico with him and he left me there. While I was hitchhiking back I met some Indian people in Arizona and went home with them. They didn't ask me any questions, just took me home and fed me, and when I wanted to talk they listened. They were a big family with an old grandmother who could easily have been my Chee-chum. I didn't stay with them very long, and when I said I was leaving, the old grandmother called me outside and slipped a handkerchief in my hand. Inside, tied in a knot, were a few crumpled old bills. She said I would need to eat.

That was the first time since I'd left home that I'd had anything to do with Native people. I'd seen many of them—mostly in Vancouver and Calgary—but I'd always made it a point to stay away from them. I knew that as long as I stayed away I would somehow always survive, because I didn't have to feel guilty about taking from white people. With my own people I would have had to share. I couldn't survive if I worried about someone else. Then there was a part of me that hated them as well. The drunken Indian men I saw would fill me with a blinding hatred; I blamed them for what had happened to me, to the little girl who had died from an overdose of drugs, and for all the girls who were on the city streets. If they had only fought back, instead of giving up, these things would never have happened. It's hard to explain how I felt. I hated our men, and yet I loved them.

When I got back to Vancouver I was back on drugs and really down and out. I moved in with an addict called Trapper and we managed to hustle enough to keep us high. We lived in a filthy little hole in a basement and came out only to find money. I was skin and bones with running sores all over my body. I was bruised and battered from the beatings I got from Trapper and whoever else felt like beating me.

Then one night I found myself thinking of Cheechum and of my childhood. I remembered her saying, "You can have anything you want if you want it bad enough." I got up and went for a walk and suddenly it was all so clear. I could quit if I made up my mind. I could leave and work on a farm, I could scrub floors—anything—I didn't have to stay here. I walked back to our room and cleaned myself up as best as I could, and then went to a small coffee shop on West Hastings and found a girl who had tried to befriend me once at Lil's. She had gone straight and was on some sort of religious kick. I told her I wanted to kick and I needed her help. She took me home and again I went through withdrawal. Although it was worse than the first time, in a way it was easier, because this time my Cheechum was with me the whole time. I could feel her presence in the room with me and I wasn't afraid.

When it was all over I phoned Ray. He came right away and again he took me home and nursed me back to health. He picked Lisa up and paid for all the months of room and board I'd missed. I told him that I wanted a job out in the country, so he called someone up and I got a job, cooking on a ranch in Alberta. The wages weren't very good, but both Lisa and I would get free room and board. They wanted me to start as soon as possible. Ray was leaving for Montreal for a couple of days and asked that I wait till he got back. I agreed and the next evening while I was putting Lisa down for the night there was a knock at the door. Before I had a chance to answer, two men walked in. When you've been in the places I've been in you know cops when you see them. They proceeded to ransack the rooms and my clothing. They asked for the keys to the car and searched it. Then they questioned me about Ray: where he was; who he was seeing; was I working for him; how long I had lived with him. I told them I knew nothing and that he was merely a friend. They laughed, then one man grabbed my arm and pulled up the sleeve of my sweater. He pulled it down after seeing the marks were not recent ones.

Ray phoned a little later and when I told him what had happened he said not to worry, he was coming back the next day. I met him at the airport and waited while he was taken to another area and searched. After he was released and we were driving into the city, I asked for the first time if they had anything on him. He answered, "Yes. There's a real crackdown in Vancouver and I'll probably be next on the list." How funny it seemed for Ray to be so concerned about me when he was going to be caught and sent up for a long stretch. I took his hand and said, "I'm really sorry." He looked at me and asked, "Do you know, that's the first time I've ever heard you say something like you really meant it? Thank you." I felt very uncomfortable, and changed the subject because whatever I felt was only for a moment.

The morning of my departure there was a knocking on the door. A man had a briefcase for me from Ray. Inside was a roll of bills and a note which said that the money would look after me for a few months in case my job didn't work out, and to put the money in a bank. There was a P.S.: "Don't worry about paying it back, it's someone else's." Ray was later picked up and given a prison sentence.

Chapter 19

Lisa and I arrived in Calgary in February of 1960. A white-haired old man in a worn-out Stetson and run-down boots met us at the airport. He seemed very surprised when he found out I was the new cook. During our drive to the ranch he volunteered some information, although he was hardly the talkative type. He said I would be cooking for anywhere from fifteen to twenty men. The ranch house was used as the headquarters and would be my home. The men used the bunkhouses. The owners lived in Calgary. He told me not to have my heart set on the job because the boss had been expecting a much older woman. I wanted to laugh; I was twenty years old but I felt like a hundred.

He asked me if I could cook and when I replied yes, he grunted and said not many women my age could. He sounded so disgusted I had to laugh. He spent the rest of the trip telling me about all the previous cooks they'd had—four this last year, and none of them could even fry an egg according to him. We arrived late in the evening, and the ranch hands were all in the kitchen drinking coffee. They looked at me and there was dead silence. They all left after Bud introduced me as the new cook. As they were going out the door I overheard one of them say, "Wow, she's too good looking to know how to cook." I thought, "I'll show them that I'm the best damned cook they've ever had!"

The house was old and very comfortable, and for a minute I felt like I was home. The kitchen was huge with an old black wood stove, a rain barrel and the biggest table I had ever seen. In the center there was a buggie wheel that held salt, pepper, jam and various other such things. Someone had rigged it up to work like a lazy-susan to save reaching. There was a small living room and two bedrooms. Bud occupied the upstairs. I made up my mind I was going to stay, and that night I cleaned the bedroom and kitchen, and got a batch of biscuits ready for mixing in the morning.

Breakfast had to be ready at six a.m., unless orders were given otherwise. There were eggs, bacon, sausages, fried potatoes and hot biscuits on the table when the men came in. No one said a word, and I watched as they started to eat. In a few minutes everyone was talking and I knew I'd passed my first test. The next test was dinner. Cal, the boss, was expected, so I really had to produce. It was a long time since I had cooked on a wood stove, and even longer since I had made bread, but I had to keep this job, so I mixed bread, put a roast on, made pies, mashed potatoes, gravy, a huge spread. The bread was baking when Cal arrived. The house was scrubbed. I was nearly dead from exhaustion and had so many burns I was smarting all over. He came to the side door, and when he saw the clean floor, took his boots off and walked in. He looked at the pies and at Lisa, and then at me. Cal said that the men were lonely, I was young and attractive, and it was a bad combination, but that he was hiring me against his better judgment. I got the job, providing I kept out of trouble. I got along well with the hands, who were more than happy to have decent meals and someone to do their laundry and mending. I cleaned and painted the house, and went out of my way to make it a home for all of us.

The country was different from my home. There were miles of bald prairie over which the wind blew endlessly. The ranch was on the banks of the Bow

River, and despite the stark landscape it had its own special beauty. Not far from the ranch house, the foreman said, was an old Blackfoot campsite considered a sacred place to the Blackfoot people. It was on a hill, and there were traces of a sundial and teepee circles. Many stories were told by the men on the ranch and people in town about the Blackfoot Indians, none of them favourable. However, once word got around that I was half Indian I never heard any more, except for the odd legend that someone remembered.

On Saturday afternoons I would go into town with the ranch hands to do my shopping, and after taking Lisa to an elderly baby-sitter, I would have a beer with the boys and go to a movie or a dance. The only close friends I made were a young couple, Ken and Sharon, who owned a small ranch.

Ken came from a large family and they all lived communally—his Mom, Dad, three sisters and six brothers and their wives. They were wild and rowdy and reminded me of my own people. The boys travelled the rodeo circuit, and when they were home for weekends it was one continuous rodeo. They owned a lot of horses and bucking stock, and would hold what they called "Jackpot Rodeos." Everybody there would put money in a hat and at the end of the day whoever had the most points would collect it all. Because of my love for horses, I was soon involved in all these gatherings. Sharon and I became close friends, the only close woman friend I had had since Karen and I were kids.

However, my troubles were soon to begin, just as in Kristen. The guys at the ranch were good to me, treating me like a kid sister and were very protective towards Lisa and me. It was easy to get along with the men at the rodeos as they respected my ability to handle horses. But I was young and attractive, with a baby and no husband. I lived alone with fifteen or twenty men and I was part Indian. I drank whiskey, drove fast, and spent a lot of time with the wildest family in the district. Soon the women were talking and the men stopped treating me like an equal, and instead became interested in me as a woman.

In Kristen I had, out of anger and frustration, deliberately given people something to talk about, but here, I was sick and tired of parties and men. I wasn't interested in any man, or for that matter, anyone period. All I wanted was to stay the hell out of trouble and be left alone. But I managed to really mess things up. I liked to gamble and played a lot of poker, not just with the men on the ranch, but with those in town as well, and I did drink a lot, and I did travel in the company of men—but only because I was comfortable with them. I found it very difficult to talk to women, in fact I was frightened to death of them. So other than Sharon I had no friends of my own sex. Once I realized people were starting to talk, I started to stay home and didn't go anywhere except to do my shopping. That was even worse, because then people said I was pregnant.

To add to my problems Cal had hired two new hands. When they arrived I was almost sick with fear. I'd met one of them somewhere. That night at supper I tried to appear calm, and once we were seated the guy asked me if I'd ever lived in Vancouver. I answered, "No, but I've been there to visit an aunt a couple of times." He remarked how much I looked like a girl he'd met there once. Then he laughed and said, "Hell, she'd never be on a ranch cooking anyway." Cal was there for supper that night and he knew I'd come from Vancouver. He casually asked what the girl had been doing? Before Ray had time to answer, Shawn, the other new guy, cut in and said how some people certainly looked alike. He knew a guy in Belfast who could have passed for Cal's twin. I could have cried I was so relieved, because then everyone started talking. Ray kept at me for nearly a week. Whenever he had a chance he'd asked me questions until I was so uptight I could hardly sleep.

Then one morning after everyone had gone to work Shawn came in. He asked me if I was the girl Ray was talking about. I said yes and I told him everything, and how I was afraid I'd end up on drugs again. I told him I needed this job, and if Cal knew he'd probably fire me because there was already enough talk. He told me not to worry, that he'd talk to Ray and straighten him out. Ray never said any more to me, but I was always afraid of him.

I liked Shawn; he was from Belfast, and had only been in Canada a short time. I'd never met a man like him in my life. He was kind, gentle and very strong. I needed strength; I was so tired of being alone with no one to ever really talk to. Shawn talked to me and gave me strength, and I guess I came as close to being in love as I could ever be. I stopped being a tough girl, and for the first time in years I felt warm and alive, but it was all over in a very short time. We came home from a wedding dance one night and there were policemen waiting for us. They grabbed Shawn, put handcuffs on him and he was gone. I was told he was wanted for murder in Belfast, and later I heard he had received a life sentence. I don't know if it was true—I never heard from him again. I was fired the following week, and if he wrote to me I never received the letters.

Chapter 20

I found a small housekeeping room in Calgary and tried to decide what I was going to do now. I looked through the paper hoping I'd find a job but there was nothing that I could do with my kind of experience or education. Then I saw an ad for a hairdressing course. I remembered the beauty shop I had always gone to when I was at Lil's and thought of how well-dressed the girls were who worked there, so I knew the pay must be good. I found a convent for Lisa, the Providence Crèche in Calgary, and paid her room and board for the six months I would be in school, and then I went out to look for part-time work.

I found one job waiting tables at the bus depot from eight in the evening till midnight. Then I found another one at the racing stable from six to eight each morning, rubbing down horses and walking them. I got up at five-thirty, went to the barns until eight, rushed home to shower and change, and got to school by nine. After studying till four o'clock, I would eat, visit Lisa or try to sleep for a couple of hours, and then go and wait tables till midnight. After about two months I felt like a walking zombie. Besides being physically exhausted, I knew that I was three months pregnant. I'd been hoping for a long time that I wasn't, and had tried not to think of it, but finally one night I just couldn't stand it anymore. I was so tired and depressed. It didn't matter how I looked at my problems, there was just no way that I could find a solution. If I stopped working, I'd have no money or food. If I stopped school, I'd have no training for a job. If I finished school, I couldn't get a job anyway because I'd be having a baby. The restaurant would fire me once I started looking pregnant, and there was just no way I could live on the money I made rubbing down horses, even if they did let me stay. All I wanted to do was lie down and sleep and never wake up again. I wrote a letter to the Sisters at the Crèche asking them to keep Lisa. I was going to commit suicide, I said, but to please not tell her how I had died. Then I went out and bought eight bottles of iodine and drank them all. Nothing happened, except that I got violently sick and ended up in the hospital, and my budget was a few dollars shorter for my trouble.

A girl with whom I had become friends visited me in hospital, and came to my room when I got back home. She said she knew someone who would give me an abortion. The woman was a former nurse and it would be a clean job. I told her I couldn't afford an abortion, but Arlene said, "The woman is my mother and she'll do it for free if I ask her."

Arlene made the arrangements for me to be at her mother's house on a Saturday night. The woman left me alone while she went into the bedroom to make preparations. While she was gone I started thinking, and I knew that I couldn't kill my baby; I would just have to find a way to manage somehow. When the woman returned she knew I had changed my mind. She came over and, putting her arm around me, said, "It's going to be hard but you can do it." We drank coffee and talked until daylight. She told me that she had been deserted by her husband and left to raise seven children, and although she was a registered nurse in a Calgary hospital, she couldn't make enough money to feed and clothe them, pay rent and a housekeeper's wages. So she had started giving abortions, but had been caught and given a six-month sentence. Her children were taken away from her and placed in foster homes and she lost her licence to nurse. When she was released she couldn't get her children back and she began to drink heavily. Since then she had been in and out of jail, mostly due to alcohol, but she had learned in prison how to avoid being caught on an abortion charge. Her children were nearly grown up now and were in all sorts of trouble. She didn't know who was to blame—herself or the Welfare Department. But she just didn't give a damn anymore. I remember sitting there with her and thinking, "Here we are, the two of us, and we weren't any different from any other women. What happened anyway? Why do we have to fight so damn hard for so little?" I wondered then if good, straight women ever experienced the torment, agony and loneliness we had to face, and if they did, how in hell did they cope?

We talked about marriage, children—all sorts of things. I guess it was the first time since I had left Cheechum that I ever talked to a woman about anything personal. At one point she said to me, "You know Maria, it takes a special kind of man to marry women like us and live with us without dragging up the past. I'm in my late forties and I've never met one yet. Maybe you will someday. I hope so, because you don't belong in this rat race." I went to bed that night thinking, "If I don't belong here, then where the hell do I belong?"

Arlene told me a few weeks later that her mother had been picked up and given a three-year sentence in Kingston Penitentiary in Ontario. I didn't see this woman again until years later, when I went as a representative of the Metis Association of Alberta to speak to the Women's Section of Fort Saskatchewan jail. She was doing two years less a day for forgery. She grabbed my hand as I walked by and said, "You made it, Maria. I knew you would." She went back to her cell before my speech was finished. She didn't want to talk to me again, and I understood.

I managed to finish the hairdressing course two months before Laurie was born, and then one of the nuns at the convent where Lisa was staying arranged a housekeeping job for me in a private home. Laurie was a beautiful baby, and for the first time in my life I prayed. I didn't know if there really was a God, but at that moment it didn't matter. I loved my baby, and though I didn't know how we were all going to survive, I was sure that somehow it would all get better.

When I was discharged from hospital I moved in with a girlfriend who had two children and was living on welfare. Marion was an Indian involved, after a fashion, with different Native activities in Calgary. I attended a couple of meetings with her but didn't go back after that. The people at those meetings reminded me of that Indian man in a suit who had come to our camp with a delegation of townspeople long ago. They seemed to me to be second-hand suits, whose owners were desperately trying to fit in, but never quite succeeding. The whites at the meetings were the kind of people who had failed to find recognition among their own people, and so had come to mine, where they were treated with the respect they felt they deserved.

I got a job in a beauty salon and started work immediately, while Marion babysat for me. Wages were very poor and after two weeks it was obvious that I would never manage on my salary. I finally went to the Welfare office because I was really desperate, and Marion had said that they had to help me and would. The social worker who talked to me was a very cold man, who, upon discovering that I had two hundred dollars, told me I had to spend it first and then come back and see him. That night Marion scolded me. "If you want help, never tell them the truth. Act ignorant, timid and grateful. They like that. Tomorrow we'll go shopping and spend the two hundred." So next morning we spent the two hundred dollars on clothes for myself and the girls. Then she

154

gave me her welfare coat, as she called it, to wear, as it was hardly appropriate to go to Welfare well dressed.

I went to the Office in a ten-year-old threadbare red coat, with old boots and a scarf. I looked like a Whitefish Lake squaw, and that's exactly what the social worker thought. He insisted that I go to the Department of Indian Affairs, and when I said I was not a Treaty Indian but a Halfbreed, he said if that was the case I was eligible, but added, "I can't see the difference—part Indian, all Indian. You're all the same." I nearly bit my tongue off sitting there trying to look timid and ignorant. I answered a hundred questions and finally he gave me a voucher for groceries and bus tickets, and told me to be sure I found a cheap apartment or house, because government money was not to be wasted. I left his office feeling more humiliated and dirty and ashamed than I had ever felt in my life.

That afternoon I said to Marion, "To hell with it. I'm not going through that business again. I'll go back on the street—at least there I'm not going to feel guilty about spending government money, and I'll be earning every cent of it." Marion tried to reason with me saying, "Once summer comes we can make a few dollars here and there. The Calgary Stampede always needs Indians. There's no need to go out and earn a living on the street. We can fix up outfits for ourselves, and go to pow wows, and put on for white people, and get paid."

I was horrified at what she was saying. I couldn't see myself in an Indian woman's costume, parading around while white people took pictures of me. I asked her if she was serious, did Indians really get paid to be Indians for tourists? Marion answered that business was good in Calgary for Indians. White people said it was a cultural thing, so no one thought it was bad.

Talking to Marion that day I saw myself wearing gaudy feathers and costumes and dancing for a place in society. To me it was the same as putting on a welfare coat to get government money. So I told her, "Forget about being a white man's Indian, and make some real money. That's the only thing this rotten world recognizes and respects."

Chapter 21

I didn't go back on the street, but I nearly did many times. The only thing that kept me away was my fear of using dope again and losing my babies for good. I stayed on welfare for six months and kept my head down, wore an old coat and acted timid and ignorant until I thought I'd go mad. Finally I couldn't stand it anymore, and told them to shove it. I found a job as a waitress in a small town south of Calgary, and managed to survive on the meagre salary I made. I found a young girl who was pregnant and had no place to go, and she babysat for her meals and a place to live. I never used dope again but I did a lot of drinking and I swallowed a lot of pills. One thing I've always found is that if you're looking for food, shelter, clothing, or just someone to talk to, there's never anyone around. But if you're looking for a party there's always lots of people who will spend a fortune seeing that you stay blissfully drunk.

I was drinking more and more all the time, but I wasn't as fortunate as many people who can get drunk and forget. Instead I'd drink myself sober and feel worse. I wanted to go home and see my father and my Cheechum. I'd never written to her or Daddy and I didn't even know if they were still alive. Sometimes when Marion would come out from Calgary to visit me, and would tell me about her family, I'd feel so lonely I'd cry.

Marion was going to AA meetings, and wanted me

to come to Calgary some weekend and go with her, but I refused. I didn't want any part of those meetings, or those people. It was bad enough that I had a drinking problem and was managing to stay off drugs—all I needed to add to my troubles was a room full of drunks. She had to be out of her mind.

My life became an endless circle of work, drink, and depression. I managed to keep food in our mouths and a roof over our heads, but that was about all.

I'd often seen Indian people in the town. Sometimes they'd come into the restaurant where I worked, but I never tried to be friendly. Most of the time they were drunk, and sometimes they would get into fights. They would leave their children in their cars, or on the street, and sit in the bar for hours. I saw white people do the same thing too, but I didn't give a damn about them. Many of the young girls came to the restaurant, and the white men would make crude jokes and try to pick them up. Many times I burned with rage and hatred, but I tried to suppress these emotions. But it was hard, and once I hit a man with a pop bottle and cut his head because he was pawing a young girl.

There was another time when two little Indian boys came in. They were about four and eight years old. The place was nearly full, and in order to reach the bathroom they had to walk the length of the restaurant. About half-way down the room sat a group of white men who had just come out of the bar, drunk and noisy. The little boys caught my eye as soon as they walked in. The mother had come in with them, but when she saw all the people she stayed outside. The children stood there, tiny, ragged, and big-eyed. They looked so much like my little brothers a lump came to my throat. As they started down the aisle one of the men yelled, "Watch it! The bow and arrows are coming." The older child stopped for a second when everyone started to laugh, put his arm around his little brother and, with his head up, continued walking.

158

The men laughed at them and the younger boy started to cry and they ran the rest of the way. I shouted at the men to stop. I was so angry I could scarcely speak. The place became very quiet. No one looked at me when I ran to the washroom and brought those little boys out. The little one was crying and I carried him out to the car. I didn't say anything to their parents—I just wanted to go away and forget the whole incident. Every so often the memory would come back of that little boy with his arm around his brother, and each time it filled me with frustration, hopelessness and despair. I could have blamed the parents for being too gutless, but how could I? Deep down inside I understood why they were afraid, because I was afraid too, only I showed my fear in a different way.

My Cheechum used to tell me that when the government gives you something, they take all that you have in return—your pride, your dignity, all the things that make you a living soul. When they are sure they have everything, they give you a blanket to cover your shame. She said that the churches, with their talk about God, the Devil, heaven and hell, and schools that taught children to be ashamed, were all a part of that government. When I tried to explain to her that our teacher said governments were made by the people, she told me, "It only looks like that from the outside, my girl." She used to say that all our people wore blankets, each in his own way. She said that other people wore them too, not just Halfbreeds and Indians, and as I grew up I would see them and understand. Someday though, people would throw them away and the whole world would change. I understood about the blanket now—I wore one too. I didn't know when I started to wear it, but it was there and I didn't know how to throw it away. So I understood about those boys' parents—it was easier for them to stay in the car. If they came out from under their blankets, they'd have to face reality, ugly as it was.

Chapter 22

One afternoon while I was working, a man came into the restaurant. His hair was black and curly, and so clean I was sure it would squeak if touched. He was very dark, sun-tanned, with white teeth and sparkling eyes. He walked like the whole world was a happy place, and he was the happiest in it. I had never met anyone like him in my life. I fell head over heels in love, and finally understood what Cheechum meant when she told me, "Someday, somewhere, you'll meet a man who'll grow old with you and you'll know him when you meet him."

His name was David, and talking with him that day I learned a little about him. He was twenty-eight and single; he had been a truck driver since he was seventeen; he liked driving. His parents were both dead and he had been on his own since the age of fifteen. He was an only child, and had no aunts, uncles—no one.

I saw David often after that. He met Lisa and Laurie, and soon he was taking us for drives and spending his free days with us. I told him that I had been married and separated, but couldn't bring myself to tell him any more. The girls loved him and I felt as though I had known him all my life and that the past was just a bad dream. His job in the town was nearly finished, and I knew he would be leaving soon, but I tried not to think about it. When he left he promised to write. He didn't know I was pregnant.

In August 1962, Robbie was born at the High River hospital. I had very little to be happy about, but I was happy when I looked at my son. The nurses took him away and I fell asleep, only to be wakened and told that my husband wanted to see me. My whole world collapsed. I didn't want to see Darrel, but there was little I could do to avoid a scene. I felt numb when I heard him coming down the hall. I looked up and David burst into the room. He said that I should have told him I was pregnant, that he loved us and that we were to go with him.

Our life was wonderful for the first few months, and in my happiness I completely forgot the past. We were living in a trailer at a construction site in northern Alberta. Spring was approaching and the job almost completed, so we prepared to move on. We moved to Leduc to another job-site. One day I picked up the newspaper and read that Lil had been arrested in Calgary, and had been put on trial. Her books had been seized, and girls who had worked for her, as well as some of her clients, were being called up as witnesses.

(I learned later that Lil died of cancer in a federal penitentiary. The real estate, race horses, and businesses that she owned in both B.C. and Alberta were taken over by many of the men who had been her clients and her business partners. She never kept anything in her own name—instead she held shares in various companies. She always believed her property would be protected if she left it in the care of influential men. Then if she were sentenced she would have money when she was released, and be able to retire.)

I was sure I would be picked up in a matter of days, and was constantly terrified. I kept the doors locked and curtains drawn when David was away, and when he was home I was a mass of nerves. I never went out of the house, and did the shopping by phone. I started to drink again, and as soon as David had gone on a trip I would phone a cab driver to pick up a bottle and deliver it to me. David knew nothing about my past, and I was so afraid he'd find out somehow. I began losing weight, and had no appetite. Finally a doctor prescribed tranquilizers and sleeping pills for me. So I was back on pills—along with the whiskey they kept me going for a while. Finally the trial ended, and I should have been able to relax, but I couldn't. I never laughed anymore, and David felt that I didn't love him. He knew I wasn't the same girl he had met, but didn't know what was the matter with me.

It's a wonder that my babies ever survived through it all. I kept them clean and fed, but I completely neglected them as far as playing with them or letting them know they were loved. Instead, Lisa would do for me what I should have been doing for them. She would come to my bed at night when she heard me crying, and hold me close, patting my shoulder and telling me, "It's OK Mommy, it's OK." Finally I made up my mind to commit suicide, and to take my children with me. I was afraid no one would want them and they would only be pushed around. One day I gave them each a sleeping pill and laid them down on the chesterfield. Then I locked the doors and windows, blew out all the pilot lights on the stove and furnace, and turned on the gas. I decided to wait for about half an hour, to be sure they all died first, before I took the rest of the sleeping pills.

Suddenly I seemed to wake up and realize what I was doing. I shut off the gas and raced around opening the doors and windows. I was sick at what I had done. I cried as I put them to bed, wondering what in god's name was wrong with me. I was determined to straighten myself out, and to stop drinking, and to get off the pills.

David was laid off at the end of October, and we moved to Edmonton. I knew I was going to crack up. I could feel a scream of hysteria bubbling up in the back of my throat, and I had to keep swallowing to keep my sanity. If it got out I would go mad. It was impossible to talk to David, because whenever we tried we could only get so far and then we'd stop. Finally we agreed to separate. On New Year's Day I felt great—packing was done and I was moving out the next morning. Everything was fine. I made some tea and sat down to drink it with David in the kitchen. I don't remember anything after that.

I came to in the Alberta Hospital two weeks later, strapped to a bed. A priest was in the room but I refused to listen to him. A doctor came around and explained that I had swallowed a lot of pills and had had a nervous breakdown. I resisted all their efforts to make me talk. All I wanted to do was shut my eyes and pretend no one was there, and that I was dead. They made me get up and walk. So long as they were around I did as I was told, but sat down as soon as they left. I had no will to do anything else.

The hospital was a dull, lifeless place. They fed us, and made sure we harmed no one, otherwise we were left alone. My "B" Ward was full of women like myself, and some who were worse off. We read, talked, knitted and played cards. Some kept apart from the rest of us. Their greatest fear was being released. They would be all right until a nurse or doctor came along, and then they would feign insanity. Sometimes they were moved to another ward, and eventually some received shock treatments. One attractive lady in her late forties had been there for over seven years. She believed she was Cleopatra, and spent hours sitting on a chesterfield. Sometimes one of us would feed her and pretend to be her slave. Sometimes she would walk about with her long hair down her back, a crown of pearl necklaces on her head, and if one of us bumped into her, she would get hysterical. Another fairly stout woman, with the most enormous belly, believed that she was going to have a baby, and would discuss her pregnancy with us. She knitted baby clothes constantly, and complained about aches and pains only pregnancies could cause. She went into labour twice while I was there, and I could have sworn she was really delivering. In the morning she had a doll beside her. The doll died the same day; she put it away and became pregnant again. One woman had huge breasts and she would stop and offer us milk shakes. Once I agreed to humour her, and she began to shake her breasts violently.

The doctor decided one day that I needed something to occupy my mind and my time, so I was sent upstairs with some other women to feed the grannies. I will never forget that room or those people for as long as I live. There was one big huge room. The walls and floor were painted grey, and tied to a number of round pillars were old women in all stages of undress. Some just sat on the floor and stared at nothing. Some played with themselves, some were crying and babbling, and some were crouched as if they were afraid they were going to be kicked. They were all skinny and whitish-looking, with stringy hair and watery eyes. The smell of urine and disinfectant was everywhere. The nurse gave us each a bowl of thick mush and a tablespoon and told us to feed them. I went to one old lady, who was slumped down on the floor, and tried to feed her. She kept choking, so I gave her small spoonfuls at a time. The nurse came by, poked me with her foot, and told me to hurry up. I started to cry, because of the hopelessness of the situation. The nurse told me to leave if I was going to get all weepy. She said, "These people don't know anything, they're vegetables." There was a woman working beside me who was calm and seemed to know what to do. She walked back to the ward with me and told me that she had been a psychiatric nurse, but was now a patient in the hospital too. She had slashed her wrists after the break-up of her marriage. She also had four children. Her name was Trixie and we became very close friends.

We didn't get much help in the hospital as none of the staff seemed to have time for the patients. The majority of them seemed as sick as their patients anyway. The doctor made only one more visit. He told me that I had to tell David the truth and make a clean break. David had been to the hospital nearly every day. I talked to David that night and told him everything. All he said was, "I've been blaming myself for your breakdown. I guess I can stop now." Then he left.

If it hadn't been for Trixie and her friendship, I would have given up completely in that place. But slowly I got better, and I started to wonder about my children. Up until then I hadn't even thought of them. The nurses all reassured me that they were fine.

I could hardly wait to get out of there. However, the doctor told me that I had to attend AA meetings before even being considered for release. So finally I gave in and went to one. The meetings were held in one of the recreation halls. All those assigned to AA were called together and led by a male orderly, followed by a nurse. We went along two by two. We walked through corridors and more corridors, and doors that had to be unlocked and locked as we passed. Six members of AA were gathered in a group when we arrived, and they introduced themselves. One man called the meeting to order by saying, "My name is John, and I'm an alcoholic." Someone from the audience read the Preamble, which starts out: "Rarely have we seen a person fail who has thoroughly followed our path. . . ." Then one by one the other outside members briefly told their life stories. They related how AA had helped them find a normal way of life, happiness, peace of mind, and self respect. I came out of the first meeting thinking, "My God, it's unbelievable." I could stop using drugs and alcohol, but I could never achieve the serenity and peace of mind that these people had found. I continued going to meetings, as it was the road to release, but paid little attention to what went on. Before permission was given to leave the hospital, the doctor warned me that if I was to survive, I would have to belong to AA the rest of my life.

I felt good and strong—no longer confused—and had gained weight during the three months of my stay. Trixie was released two days before me, and we planned to join forces and start again. At the hospital they gave me a new hair-do, returned my clothes and personal things, and gave me my Family Allowance of eighteen dollars. That was all the money I had when I left.

My first couple of weeks flew by. I visited Virginia, who ran the local AA office, and met Don, who became my sponsor. Whenever I got mixed up I called Don, and he would come right over—which seemed like every four hours. He took me home, and I met his wife Edith. She was part Indian, young looking, friendly but brisk, with a no-nonsense attitude about her. I liked her instantly and we became good friends. She helped me as much as Don, and even more. She helped me to get over my mental block about Indians in suits—perhaps not completely, but at least so that their ways no longer upset me. She taught me to look at myself as critically as I looked at them, and to believe that the same thing that drove me, drove them to being what they were, that basically we had all suffered trouble and misery, and that their problems were as big and as important as mine, regardless of how unimportant I thought they were. She was very honest, almost to the point of hurting me, while Don was very easy, and consoled me, and was very careful not to upset me.

Because of Edith I began to understand what Cheechum had been trying to say to me, and to see how I had misinterpreted what she had taught me. She had never meant that I should go out into the world in search of fortune, but rather that I go out and discover for myself the need for leadership and change: if our way of life were to improve I would have to find other people like myself, and together try to find an alternative. Edith had grandparents like my Cheechum, so she understood, and tried to explain it to me realistically. Because of her I eventually attended meetings at the Native Friendship Center. She said that if I was ever going to become strong inside, I would have to face reality.

I joined an AA group I liked and attended meetings regularly. It was a mixture of real down-and-outers, some white, some Native, drunks from skidrow, ex-cons from various institutions and women like myself. It was good: I understood these people, and they understood me. It was here that I first met the people that would play an important role in the Native movement in Alberta.

Chapter 23

One of these people was Eugene Steinhauer. He had nothing when he came to AA except the clothes on his back. He had lived on various skid-rows and his family had given him up as a derelict. Now he was finding sobriety, as well as hope for himself, and a future as something more than just another drunken Indian. I admired him because he was the first Indian I had ever met who let white people know how he felt about them, not just by his attitude, but verbally as well. I'd hated those nameless, faceless white masses all my life, and he said all the things I had kept bottled up inside for so many years.

At this time, I felt Eugene could do no wrong. He was one of the "brothers" Cheechum had talked about. When, following his example, I too began to speak out, his attitude towards me changed. At the time I was hurt and discouraged because to me he was a special person, but it doesn't matter anymore. Since then I've met many Native leaders who have treated me the same and I've learned to accept it. I realize now that the system that fucked me up fucked up our men even worse. The missionaries had impressed upon us the feeling that women were a source of evil. This belief, combined with the ancient Indian recognition of the power of women, is still holding back the progress of our people today.

But then I met Stan Daniels, a Halfbreed from St. Paul, Alberta. He was one of many children in a famíly raised on bannock, rabbits and tea. The French kids used to kick his ass home from school, as he said, and his sanctuary was a sixteen by twenty-four-foot mud shack where he'd hide and cover his ears from the taunts of *"Sauvage! Sauvage!"* He had never slept in a bed until he joined the Army at sixteen.

Stan was married and had a very close relationship with his family. He could feel people's needs, whether it was an empty space inside oneself or the need for fun. He was both compassionate and tough. Being with him brought back memories of Jim Brady, my childhood, and my people, for he was a Halfbreed through and through. He could sit down at his table with authority, his wife and children around him, and the room full of noisy, shouting people. He would eat up food as if there would be none tomorrow, slurping up coffee, belching, children climbing all over him, shrieking and laughing. The whole room would revolve around him and there would always be lots of music.

Stan didn't get involved in the same way as Eugene and some of the others who were involved at this time. He was really concerned about the plight of Native girls on the street. He was bitter about what the white system had done to our men, causing them to leave their women. He understood how the men in prison felt—it was good to get temporary relief away from their problems. He understood how women ended up on the street, and the things that they could not talk about, and how the Indian women felt about being abandoned by their men.

This man was to play a traumatic role in my life and in the lives of Native people in Alberta and Canada. He worked to draw attention to the plight of Native people and motivated many others to do something as well. As government money became available, as well as public recognition, the seemingly inevitable changes which come to leaders happened.

Today, although Stan and I each go our separate

ways, he is still an important person to me, and I love him as a brother. Sometimes I feel sorry for him. I know that he sees what is wrong, but he can't or won't do anything to try to change it. Maybe he's just too tired to continue. The pain I feel is without the bitterness I felt as a young idealistic Native woman, and I don't blame him. I can only hate the system that does this to people.

About this same time I met Gilbert Anderson, and a little later, his wife, Kay. Gilbert was quiet, calm and radiated warmth and friendliness. He too was a Halfbreed. Kay was someone I could talk to about babies and diapers, as well as world affairs. Cheechum used to tell me when I complained about women, "You have many sisters out there, my girl. You'll find them." Kay became one of my sisters. Over the years Gilbert and Kay and I have remained close friends, despite some differences of opinion, and my respect and admiration for both of them is strong.

I was starting to get on my feet again. I had a job in a restaurant and the children were in a foster home. I had met their foster parents who were a warm and understanding older couple. When they found out I was living in a little housekeeping room, they took me under their wing as well, and treated me like a daughter. They're still good friends today.

I'd never heard from David since the day we talked at the hospital, and had pushed him completely out of my mind. I didn't expect to ever see him again.

During this time I began writing to AA inmates at Prince Albert Penitentiary. Within two months I had more mail than I ever had in my whole life. It was hard to know what to write about, so I wrote about the children, my job and my problems, my frustrations and hopes. They answered every week, and soon it was as if we had known each other all our lives. They blasted me, gave me advice and encouragement, and the concerns of my home and children became

170

theirs. When I wrote to tell them that the children had come to live with me again, they had a celebration.

Then one day an invitation came to attend a conference at the prison. I was excited because it meant that, while on the trip, I could also go home and see Daddy, Cheechum, and maybe my brothers and sisters.

When I arrived at the prison, the guys overwhelmed me and asked about Robbie, and how Lisa was doing in school, and about Laurie. Later at the meeting, I listened as each speaker gave his story. They spoke about the homes and families they had lost, and how they hoped they would be able to go straight outside and rebuild their lives. When the chairman thanked the speakers, he added that a presentation was to be made to a very special person. He said that many of the men were serving life sentences, some had been in and out for years and had lost track of their families, or had none. They looked forward to getting news of someone's garden, or a little boy having his first fight, or little girls going to their first party. He said that here in Prince Albert they were lucky because they had a family and the best-looking and most mixed-up broad in the world. She was a little girl who could sew, plant a garden, play poker and cuss. Then he asked if I would come up to the platform.

They gave me a painting, and said it was from all of them to me and my children. The painting was of a burnt-out forest, all black, bleak and dismal. In the center was a burnt-out tree stump, and at the roots were little green shoots sprouting up. The forest was like our lives, and the shoots represented hope.

There was one old man in his late sixties who looked and talked like someone in an old Al Capone movie. He was one of the first prisoners sentenced to the Penitentiary when it was opened. He told me that he had not heard from his family for some twenty years. When I was leaving, he took my hand and said,

"Maria, I've never had children and I've never thought much about them in here, as it only adds to the problems, but if I'd ever had a daughter I would have wished for one like you. You're a good girl." I wrote to him for two years, and when he was finally released in 1967, after serving thirty years for armed robbery, he came to visit me before returning home to rebuild his life.

That evening after the conference, I phoned my aunt and learned that Daddy was home in Spring River. I got there about five in the morning, and as I approached the settlement I tried to find something that was familiar in the land around me. The old log houses were gone and in their place grew wild rose bushes. The store looked grey and desolate, and the trees that I remembered were all dried up. In the early morning light, our house—the house I had missed so much—looked lonely and dilapidated. Through the window I saw Daddy sitting alone at the table, eating breakfast.

When I walked inside, he looked at me for the longest time, and then said, "My girl! You're home!"

We spent the whole morning and early afternoon talking. He told me that during the last year he had been allowed to visit the children. Dolores and Peggie were living in a small town and were in high school, and the little boys were on a farm about twenty miles from Prince Albert. Robbie, who had been a real thorn in the side of Welfare because of his rebellious behavior, was somewhere in Alaska. They had finally left him alone after placing him in fifteen foster homes. Jamie was living in B.C., married with three children. Dad asked me why I had never written, and I replied that there had been nothing good to write home about. He didn't ask anything else, and I have never told him what happened.

That afternoon I walked around the old tumble-down houses. Grannie Campbell's was gone, but the delphiniums she loved still grew by the ruins where the kitchen once stood. I went to the cemetery and sat on old Wolverine's grave. Later on I went in to St. Michel, and because it was Saturday night it seemed as if the pages had been turned back. Only now it was worse, like a nightmare too horrible to forget. The streets were full of Native people in all stages of intoxication. There were children running everywhere; babies crying with nobody to care for them. A man was beating his wife behind a building, while little children looked on as though it was all quite normal. The only bar in town was full of people so drunk they couldn't walk. They were allowed to stay inside until their money was gone, and then they were cut off. Some of the men had dirty bandages on their faces, others had open, swollen infected cuts. There were drunken women with faces badly scarred and bruised from numerous beatings. The old angry bitter feeling came back to my stomach—the feeling of hate—as I saw people whom I had known as a child, now with such empty, despairing faces.

As I left the bar, a man took my arm, and only when he smiled, did I recognize Smoky. Over coffee he told me a little of his life. He had never married, although he was living with a white woman and her sister. He laughed when he told me that, saying, "You remember how the white people used to hate us? Well, they've got Halfbreed grandchildren all over now. Times have changed here, Maria, even the whites have deteriorated, or I guess perhaps their deterioration shows now."

Smoky and I drove around visiting friends and family. The homes were the same—one-roomed log houses, ten to sixteen children, dogs and skinny horses. But something had changed. The gentle mothers of my childhood were drunkards now, and neglect was evident everywhere, most of all on the faces of the children. The countryside had changed too. Fires had swept through parts of it, often deliberately set by men out of work and money. Welfare was cut off in the summer months, but the Forestry Department paid wages for fighting fires. There was nothing left to hunt or trap, and only Daddy still trapped in the National Park.

Smoky said, "The important thing now is getting enough money squeezed out of Welfare to buy flour, lard, tea and wine—food for the kids, and wine for us to forget we exist." When I drove him home, his blonde-haired wives came out and listened to him say to me, "Hell, some of us are lucky enough to have a white woman to make us feel we've moved up." I went home, feeling like I wanted to get Daddy's rifle and go out and shoot everything.

The following winter Daddy wrote that Smoky had shot the two white women and then killed himself.

Daddy and I went to visit Cheechum, who lived with her nephew and his wife. Driving into the yard was like old times. In the yard was a rack with meat hanging from it and a small fire burning underneath. I ran into the little log house and sitting on her pallet on the floor was my Cheechum. She hadn't changed at all. She got up when I came inside and before there was a chance to say anything she hit me with her cane. She ordered me to get out until I had covered my legs—did I have no shame at all? I backed out of the door, remembering that I was wearing shorts. Luckily there was a skirt among my clothes in the car.

Once inside the house again, Cheechum told me to come to her. She reached up and touched my face, then patted a place for me to sit beside her. We sat there for a long time, just the two of us. The tidy cabin and the familiar smell of herbs and roots and wood-smoke, and the rabbit soup simmering on the stove, all made me feel like I had come home again. We didn't have to talk—Cheechum understood my feelings. After supper we went out and walked to the lake where we sat and listened to the frogs singing, and had a smoke. She asked me then what had happened, and I told her everything that I could never have told my father. When I had finished, she said, "It's over now. Don't let it hurt you. Since you were a baby you've had to learn the hard way. You're like me." When I replied, "There's nobody I'd rather be like than you," she smiled and said, "I wonder if that's so good."

I told her about the Native people in AA, and she wanted to know all about them, especially Stan Daniels. I told her of my work with girls on the street and how I was trying to establish a halfway house where girls could come when they were in trouble. I explained that I didn't believe I could help anyone solve their personal problems, but if I could give them a home and friendship, then they would in turn find their own answers. She said, "I'm glad you believe that, and I hope you will never forget it. Each of us has to find himself in his own way and no one can do it for us. If we try to do more we only take away the very thing that makes us a living soul. The blanket only destroys, it doesn't give warmth. But you will understand that better as you get older."

Cheechum was one hundred and four years old. She was still strong, although her eyesight was failing. She told me that she was getting tired and that she was ready to go at any time. She hoped it wouldn't be too much longer. When we left, she stood outside her little log house and waved—a little lady with long white braids, a bright scarf and long black dress, jewellery on her neck and arms, feet in tiny beaded moccasins.

Daddy came back to Prince Albert with me and made arrangements at the Welfare Department for the children to come to town. Dolores was as tall as I was and looked just like Mom: she was quiet and gentle. Peggie was barely five feet tall, with red hair and freckles, and a bubbling personality. They were seventeen and fifteen. The little boys had not changed much, only grown a little taller. They cuddled up to me, sang songs, and showed off their magic tricks. They were lonely and wanted so desperately to be loved.

Chapter 24

When I came back from Saskatchewan, the horrible conditions of my people and my talk with Cheechum made me feel there was no time to waste. The more I became involved in street work the angrier I became. At one meeting I talked to the AA group about a half-way house for women. I expounded at great length that there were soup kitchens, flop houses and hostels for men throughout Canada. Furthermore, society didn't deal with men on the street as harshly as it did with women. One of the male members said that my problem was that I hated men and that probably what I needed was a good lay. I got so mad and frustrated I walked out.

That evening I met Marie Smallface, a Blood woman from Cardston. It's hard to describe her—for here was no ordinary Indian, let alone Indian woman. She was a militant and a radical long before we were saying those words in Alberta. She lived a completely free life. Knowing her made a big difference to me and brought a change in my life. She had just returned from a workshop in Banff for young Native people from across Canada, and she talked excitedly about what could happen through the Canadian Indian Youth Council. She introduced me to many young Indian people who had been involved with it. Listening to her talk, it seemed to me that here was a whole new breed of Native people who would make changes and give leadership.

Marie was good for me, and through her I began to see a lot of things differently. I met students from other countries. I listened to everything they said, and brought home piles of books to read until late at night. I never joined in the rap sessions because I was terrified to open my mouth and make a fool of myself. They used words unknown to me, and sounded so sure of themselves and their position in the world as revolutionaries. I didn't even know what that word meant, and felt that my experience and knowledge were so limited I would be like a child joining in.

There were times when it was hard to keep quiet because I didn't agree with what they were saying, but I would be lost in their flow of words. Many of the books were difficult to understand, and I would read them over and over again and be just as confused. Marie would explain what some things meant, but it made little sense. Finally, I got rid of the books: the Russian Revolution wasn't important to me anyway. Instead I started reading Canadian and Indian history.

During this time Community Development and Jim Whitford were being talked about. I didn't see how a government organization headed by a middle-class white man could do anything for Indian people, and was even more disillusioned to learn that Native people would be on the staff. To me it was Saskatchewan, the CCF party and its projects all over again. Whenever they hired Natives to work with Native people, it ended in disaster, with our people being hurt. I remembered how our people were divided and fought each other once their leaders had been hired by the government. This is how my father was beaten.

David and I were together again and were trying to straighten out our lives and start anew. I was free of drugs and alcohol, and my children were well adjusted and happy. Then Lee was born in February 1966 and for the first time in years, we were really happy.

Marie dropped in for tea one afternoon and announced that she had jobs for both of us, beginning in May. She said that Premier Manning was paying good wages for a research project in the poverty areas of Alberta, in both Native and white communities. We would be going to the Saddle Lake Reserve in central Alberta. The wages were five hundred dollars per month from May until August. I couldn't believe what I heard—to be paid that kind of wage with no experience! Marie laughed and said, "Don't worry about not knowing what to do because you've probably got more experience than they have. Besides, the whole project is going to end up in someone's back room like all the other research material anyway."

My first impression of Saddle Lake was that of rich farm land, and if the government considered this a poverty area, what did they call the really poor areas in Alberta? Once we had paid our visits to the Chief and Councillors and the R.C. priest, we started work. The questionnaire was unbelievable. It was lengthy, with a lot of ridiculous stuff, and the people being questioned would look at each other as if to say, "They must be mad." However they were friendly and patient, and answered all the questions as best they could. Many times my neck would grow hot when driving away, as we could hear their laughter, and knew that we were the joke.

After about a week, the novelty began to wear off. The other co-worker was Milt, a political science student, and he didn't get along with Marie. I was caught right in the middle, with loyalty to Marie on one side, and a big concern to save face for all of us in the community and do a good job on the other. By now I was feeling like some sort of messiah; these poor people's future rested on the results of our work. I tried to talk to Marie but she became angry, and about the middle of July she was replaced. I could leave too and keep her friendship, or shut up and finish the work. I decided to shut up, but I will be very

179

honest about my motive, as I've seen the same thing destroy so many good people in the last few years. I had never in my life felt so important, and I liked the feeling; in fact it was like I had just drunk a half bottle of whiskey. It took me two years to finish that bottle, and I was on the biggest ego and power trip any human being could be on.

The job at Saddle Lake was never finished as planned. A report was compiled on the incomplete material we had gathered, and when it was made public, the people at Saddle Lake were very upset. The headlines in the paper said, "The anatomy of a sick Reserve called Saddle Lake." That was my first experience as a scab. At the time I loved it: I was important, and I had helped to make Manning's White Paper possible.

I look back on this experience now with bitterness. Marie and I had been manipulated and divided just as my father and those leaders from my childhood had been. Although it was done in a more sophisticated way, the end result was the same, and today, when we should be working together, our feelings keep us apart.

The last week of the research project was spent in the sugar-beet fields in southern Alberta interviewing the people of Saddle Lake, who were working there for the summer months. I had asked Stan Daniels to come and help me finish off the project. We'd been told that all welfare was cut off on the Reserve and that people were forced to go to work in the fields. In order to make enough money to live they had to take their children out of school and work them as well.

Although I had heard stories of the beet fields, I was not prepared for what we saw that Saturday afternoon. Lethbridge was overflowing with Native people from Saskatchewan, Alberta, B.C. and even the States. There was a lot of drinking, the place was full of police and the jails were full. Lethbridge, like
180

towns everywhere with a large Native population, is really racist, and although it accepts Native money, it in no way accepts Native people. We walked around in the evening and saw people being thrown out of bars or being refused service in restaurants.

On Sunday it was the same, only now bootleggers were doing a thriving business everywhere, while the good people of the town hurried off to church. Monday we drove out to the beet fields, and the conditions we saw were unbelievable. Some of the houses couldn't even be called shacks. Some families lived in old granaries that were clustered around the edges of barnyards. The roofs leaked in the rain, the yards were mires of mud, cow dung and filthy water. The one-roomed granaries and shacks housed whole families, sometimes two. When the rain stopped, the heat brought out huge flies in droves.

The workers in the fields talked to us readily about conditions there. They said some of them were brought from their home areas in large buses. The drivers would stop and herd them all out every so many miles so that they could relieve themselves at the side of the roads. There was no privacy from each other or from traffic passing by on the flat prairie. The bosses shortchanged them on the work, and food prices were sky-high because they had to buy canned goods that were quick to prepare and would not spoil in the heat. If they complained they were fired. The bosses who had large crews also had their own commissaries, so that when it was time to pay the crews, a third of their wages went to pay the bills they owed.

The whole sugar-beet area was the same. The car lots sold cars to Native people at high prices, and they broke down in a couple of weeks. The money the workers made never left the community. We could not even scratch the surface of the problem in a week. A report was made, but very little was ever said about it in public. It was too ugly.

When we got back, Stan became very involved with the proposed Alberta Native Federation, thinking that through this organization he would be able to see justice done. I went to many of their meetings, but my concerns for Native people in the city did not fit in with their immediate plans, and then too, women were not encouraged to attend unless a secretary was needed.

Eugene Steinhauer, Jack Bellerose and Jim Ducharme, with the help of Community Development, drew up a proposal to be presented to the Indian reserves and Metis colonies. The idea was to use the Saul Alinsky tactic of strength in numbers and speak to government with one voice. The proposal for a federation was rejected by the Treaty Indians. They felt that the militant stand that would be taken by such an organization would jeopardize their Treaty rights. "The Halfbreeds," they said, "have nothing to lose, so they can afford to be militant."

In spite of this setback many things began to happen. The existing, but dormant Native organizations, founded by Jim Brady and Malcolm Norris in the 1920's, were reorganized. The Metis Association of Alberta elected Stan Daniels as their leader, and the Indian Association elected Harold Cardinal. These two groups were to be the political arm and voice for their people. The long-range plan, said the leaders, was that through education the people themselves would see the need for unity, thus making a federation possible. The general unrest among poor people throughout Canada could lead to a united voice on many issues affecting both whites and Natives.

Eugene founded the Alberta Native Communications Society, which managed the Cree radio program and a monthly newspaper to keep the people informed and aware.

It was all wonderful and exciting. The meeting halls in the Native communities were full and overflowing when the leaders came. People didn't kowtow to the white civil servants on reserves and colonies anymore. They started talking back. There was a new feeling of pride and hope everywhere.

The Native movement grew in strength, not just here in Alberta, but across Canada. Community Development, the organization that government had created to keep white radicals busy, suddenly became very threatened. Their objective had been to phase themselves out when Native people no longer needed them. Native people didn't need them anymore and said so. Suddenly their priority became survival. There were thousand-dollar-a-month jobs at stake if these Natives meant business. The Native leaders, whom Community Development had handpicked—and underestimated—would not be dictated to any more. Government, seeing the handwriting on the wall, phased out Community Development and gave us money. Not very much, just enough to divide us again.

The blanket that our leaders almost threw away suddenly started to feel warm again, and they wrapped it tightly around them. Those of us who saw what was happening and spoke out against it were phased out and branded as communists.

One spring day, in May of 1966, I got a phone call from my father. Cheechum had fallen from a runaway horse and buggy and had died almost immediately. He wanted me to come home for the funeral, but I didn't go. All the things that were happening in Alberta were the things she had waited eighty years for, and I knew that she would have wanted me to stay in Alberta and continue working with the movement.

Cheechum lived to be a hundred and four years old, and perhaps it's just as well that she died with a feeling of hope for our people; that she didn't share the disillusionment that I felt about the way things turned out. My Cheechum never surrendered at Batoche: she only accepted what she considered a dishonourable truce. She waited all her life for a new generation of people who would make this country a better place to live in.

For these past couple of years, I've stopped being the idealistically shiny-eyed young woman I once was. I realize that an armed revolution of Native people will never come about; even if such a thing were possible what would we achieve? We would only end up oppressing someone else. I believe that one day, very soon, people will set aside their differences and come together as one. Maybe not because we love one another, but because we will need each other to survive. Then together we will fight our common enemies. Change will come because this time we won't give up. There is growing evidence of that today.

The years of searching, loneliness and pain are over for me. Cheechum said, "You'll find yourself, and you'll find brothers and sisters." I have brothers and sisters, all over the country. I no longer need my blanket to survive.

Other Goodread Biographies you'll enjoy

In this series you'll find the stories of Canadians of all kinds — writers, artists, sports figures, nurses and doctors, adventurers...

Books that were successes in hardcover are made available in paperback in this series. You'll find them interesting and enjoyable to read — that's why we call them Goodread Biographies!

An Arctic Man by Ernie Lyall
Sixty-five years in Canada's north — by a man who chose the Inuit way of life.

Boys, Bombs and Brussels Sprouts by Doug Harvey
A huge success in hardcover, the lively story of a young Canadian pilot in war-torn Britain.

Canadian Nurse in China by Jean Ewen
The memoirs of a remarkable young woman who travelled to China with Dr. Norman Bethune.

E.P. Taylor by Richard Rohmer
The story of one of Canada's richest and most successful businessmen, by best-selling novelist-lawyer Richard Rohmer.

The Fighting Fisherman: Yvon Durelle by Raymond Fraser
An unusual sports biography — the glamourous and the seamy sides of boxing described with rare honesty.

Half-breed by Maria Campbell
A powerful book by a young Métis woman whose story of growing up with the "Road Allowance people" in northern Saskatchewan is unforgettable.

Hockey is a Battle by Punch Imlach and Scott Young
One of the game's great coaches tells the lively story of his first 30 years in hockey. A huge bestseller!

Hugh MacLennan by Elspeth Cameron
A best-selling account of one of the great Canadian writers of the century.

Letters from a Lady Rancher by Monica Hopkins
The delightful adventures of a young woman who marries a homesteader and starts a new life in the West.

Louis 'David' Riel by Thomas Flanagan
A fascinating new biography of the great Métis leader — his personal, political, and religious life.

The Making of a Secret Agent by Frank Pickersgill
The compelling story of a young Canadian who abandons pacifism to become a spy.

Morgentaler by Eleanor Wright Pelrine
The surprising life story of the controversial Montreal doctor.

Nathan Cohen by Wayne Edmonstone
The life of Canada's most passionate, most successful critic of arts and entertainment.

The Patricks by Eric Whitehead
A four-generation family of Irish-Canadians from the Ottawa Valley who made hockey history in Ontario, B.C. and the U.S.

Shaking It Rough: A Prison Memoir by Andreas Schroeder
A fresh look at life 'inside' Canada's prison system by a fine young writer who has no axes to grind.

Something Hidden: Wilder Penfield by Jefferson Lewis
The story of the world-famous Canadian surgeon and scientist.

My Uncle, Stephen Leacock by Elizabeth Kimball
A young girl's memories of summers at the lake with

Canada's most famous humourist and the whole Lea-cock clan.

Tommy Douglas by Doris French Shackleton
The story of one of the most admired — and most successful — politicians of the century.

Troublemaker! by James Gray
Western Canada's best-loved historian chronicles the golden age of the prairies from 1936 to 1955.

Walter Gordon: A Political Memoir
A gentle, passionate patriot's story of his experiences inside official Ottawa in the St. Laurent-Pearson era.

Wheel of Things: Lucy Maud Montgomery by Mollie Gillen
An intimate look at the writer who created Canadian fiction's most memorable young character, Anne of Green Gables.

When I Was Young by Raymond Massey
One of Canada's best-known actors recounts his youth as a Massey, the most "establishment" of Canadian families.

Within the Barbed Wire Fence by Takeo Nakarto
The moving story of a young Japanese man, torn from his family in 1942 and sent to a labour camp in the B.C. interior.